BRIDGES
TO ACADEMIC WRITING

BRIDGES
TO ACADEMIC WRITING

ANN O. STRAUCH
El Camino College

CAMBRIDGE
UNIVERSITY PRESS

PUBLISHED BY THE PRESS SYNDICATE OF THE UNIVERSITY OF CAMBRIDGE
The Pitt Building, Trumpington Street, Cambridge, United Kingdom

CAMBRIDGE UNIVERSITY PRESS
The Edinburgh Building, Cambridge CB2 2RU, UK
40 West 20th Street, New York, NY 10011–4211, USA
477 Williamstown Road, Port Melbourne, VIC 3207, Australia
Ruiz de Alarcón 13, 28014 Madrid, Spain
Dock House, The Waterfront, Cape Town 8001, South Africa

http://www.cambridge.org

First published by St. Martin's Press, Inc. 1997
7th printing 2004

Printed in the United States of America

Library of Congress Cataloging-in-Publication Data Available

ISBN 0 521 65795 4 Student's Book
ISBN 0 521 65794 6 Instructor's Manual

Acknowledgments are given on page 241.

CONTENTS

TO THE INSTRUCTOR

STUDENT AUDIENCE

Bridges to Academic Writing is intended for high-beginning to low-intermediate ESL composition students. It is specifically geared toward students who need to (1) develop process writing skills, (2) become familiar with common methods of organizing ideas, and (3) practice writing in response to reading prompts. These skills will prepare students for more advanced courses in higher education.

APPROACH

This text focuses first and foremost on a process approach to writing. Process writing evolved as a welcome improvement over the rhetorical modes approach, with its over-focus on the product. In their enthusiasm to embrace this new approach, however, many textbook authors minimized or omitted discussions of organizational patterns.

A process approach need not exclude the basic organizational patterns commonly used by writers of English. In fact, non-native speakers of English, perhaps even more than native speakers, need explicit guidelines for organizing their ideas in accordance with the common conventions of the English-speaking world.

Instructors help their students by making basic organizational patterns explicit and by presenting them as common patterns. These patterns are not meant to be rigid and confining but are intended to facilitate clear communication and to help students to produce successful compositions that meet the expectations of the English-speaking academic community.

The students' intuitive grasp of English writing conventions will eventually allow them to develop beyond the basic patterns presented in this text.

SCOPE OF THE MATERIAL

Bridges to Academic Writing presents the short composition consisting of one or more paragraphs. It is designed for a course one level below the course that teaches the essay.

One line of thought is that in this pre-essay course, students should be limited to writing single paragraphs. In my opinion, limiting students to one paragraph is artificial and unnecessarily restrictive. On the other hand, it is not within the scope of this pre-essay course to present introductory paragraphs, supporting paragraphs, and concluding paragraphs.

The term "short composition" is a workable alternative to the traditional concepts of "paragraph" or "essay." It gives students greater latitude to develop their ideas within a less restrictive format.

The "short composition" is similar in structure to the traditional paragraph in that it starts with a main idea, provides support, and ends with a conclusion. In some cases, the short composition may consist of only one paragraph.

If, however, the composition becomes lengthy, it may be broken into several paragraphs. In this instance, the short composition may appear visually identical to the traditional essay, but it will not necessarily contain the traditional essay parts. (If a student produces the traditional essay parts, for example, an introduction before the main idea — thesis statement — this variation is to be applauded.)

Traditionally, the term "topic sentence" refers to a piece of writing that consists of one paragraph, and the term "thesis statement" refers to a piece of writing that consists of several paragraphs. During the development of this text, it was determined that neither of these two terms was appropriate for describing the main idea of a short composition. Thus, the term "main idea" is used rather than "topic sentence" or "thesis statement."

How to Use This Text

The main instructional material appears in the following sections:

> *Getting Started*
> Section 1 — *Composing: The Basics*
> Section 2 — *Composing: Responding to Outside Sources*
> Section 3 — *Supplementary Material for Refining Skills*

Instructors may find it useful to begin teaching in the *Getting Started* section. This section introduces the concept of the "short composition," followed by a brief overview of process writing, and ends with paragraph basics. It also includes suggestions for using a computer for writing compositions.

Sections 1 and 2 (Chapters 1 to 9) comprise the core of the course. They may be covered either sequentially or on a pick-and-choose basis.

Section 1 focuses on becoming familiar with basic organizational patterns and on writing from personal experience. In addition to using personal experience, students also write in response to the writing of others.

Section 2 focuses on reading outside sources and writing summaries and responses based on the readings. In their responses, students are not limited to specific organizational patterns. Thus, as students progress in the course, the focus shifts from more-controlled to less-controlled organization, as well as from personal experience to summary and response.

Each chapter in Section 1 and Section 2 starts out with four or five sample compositions, most of them adaptations of compositions by ESL students. In *Looking at Content and Organization* and in *Practicing What You Have Learned*, students will examine the main idea, the body, and the conclusion. A section called *Language Tips* is included in Chapters 2 through 9. In *Your Turn to Write* students are taken through process writing, step by step. *Ideas for Writing* sections appear at the end of the chapters.

In contrast to Section 1 and 2, Section 3 — *Supplementary Material for Refining Skills* (Parts 1 to 7) — is not intended to be covered sequentially after Section 2. Instead, Section 3 provides supplementary discussion and practice on basic concepts.

Students are best served when they begin writing compositions as soon as possible. Since this supplementary material on refining skills is removed from the basic flow of the chapters, instructors can incorporate selected refining skills after the foundations for process writing have been firmly laid. It cannot be emphasized enough that these refinement skills are to be woven into a course according to the instructor's assessment of the needs of each specific teaching-learning situation.

The appendices contain several resources for reference. The most extensive, *Appendix 2: Process Writing,* is a compilation of the steps and activities presented in this text. By referring to this appendix, students can see how all of the pieces fit together. They can also refer to it to review a given step or activity.

Appendix 4: Grammar Highlights is not meant to comprise the entire grammar component in a composition class. For a complete treatment of grammar for composition at this level, see *Nitty Gritty Grammar* by A. Robert Young and Ann O. Strauch.

Acknowledgments

I would like to thank the following reviewers for their contributions to the book:

Tess Ferree, American Language Program, Columbia University; Kate Garretson, Central Missouri State University; Denis A. Hall, New Hampshire College, ALCC; Suzanne Leibman, College of Lake County; Elizabeth Lara, Norwalk Community Technical College; Ronald Ling, Midwest College; Judith Lynn Paiva, Northern Virginia Community College; Dr. Mary Ellen Ryder, Boise State University; Joye Smith, Hunter College-CUNY; M. E. Sokolik, UC Berkeley; and Dr. Ann Wintergerst, St. John's University.

TO THE STUDENT

WRITING FOR COLLEGE AND UNIVERSITY COURSES: PROCESS WRITING

Throughout your college/university experience, you will have to write many papers. You will write some compositions during a limited time period, often during one class session. Other compositions will take several days to complete. Still others, such as research papers, will take several weeks or several months to complete. No matter what kind of paper you write, you will find that process writing skills are essential. This text will help you learn and practice process writing.

POINTS TO KEEP IN MIND

You may be nervous at the beginning of a writing course, especially when your course is taught in a second language. This is normal. If you keep the following points in mind, you will enjoy the class more and make greater progress.

1. Your ideas. The goal in this course is to help you express your ideas in writing and begin to develop the skills that you will need in academic settings. The ideas you express will come from personal experience, discussions with others, or written resources.

2. The importance of reading. You need to read extensively in English in order to become a good writer. The fact is that students who read regularly in English make much greater progress than those who do not. Through reading, you gain ideas, vocabulary, grammar skills, organizational skills, and an intuitive feel for English.

3. Developing thinking skills. You need to challenge and stretch your thinking skills in order to learn to write well. To be more specific, you have to develop ideas, organize them, and evaluate them for their effectiveness. When you practice these kinds of thinking skills, you will be practicing the kinds of skills that will help you in other areas of your life — both academic and personal.

4. Discomfort in the early weeks of a writing course. You may feel uncomfortable in the first several weeks of the course. You may feel that you have so much to say but don't possess the English vocabulary or sentence skills to express yourself fully. This is a normal feeling, one that will lessen as you gain more experience in writing.

5. *The myth of perfection.* Nobody's writing is perfect — in any language! Even professional writers, writing in their native language, fall far short of perfection. So, think of it this way: If professional writers are not perfect, you certainly do not have to be perfect either! All you need to focus on is progress, not perfection.

6. *The role of grammar.* Using standard grammar is important, but you need to keep grammar in proper perspective. A paper that has nothing to say in terms of content is not a successful paper, no matter how perfect the grammar is. Your primary goal as a writing student is to have something to say, and to say it as clearly as possible.

7. *Prioritizing your grammar weaknesses.* Not all grammar concepts are equally important, especially in the early stages of learning to write. Do not try to attack every grammar problem that appears in your writing. This misguided strategy will simply limit your overall progress. To use your time more effectively, identify your weaknesses, prioritize them, and then concentrate on how to overcome them, a few at a time.

8. *The path to success.* Writing does not have to be an unpleasant task, but it does take some time and effort. Of course, achieving any important goal usually requires an investment of time and effort. With this in mind, if you do your best in this course, you will be well on your way to becoming a successful writer. Once you develop self-confidence based on your successes, you will discover that expressing your thoughts and ideas clearly can be richly rewarding.

"Non Sequitur" by Wiley. © 1996, Washington Post Writers Group. Reprinted with permission.

GETTING STARTED

THE SHORT COMPOSITION

In this text, you will practice writing short compositions. A short composition states and develops one main idea. It may have one or more paragraphs, as in the following examples.

Example 1

This sentence states the main idea. This sentence presents a supporting point. This sentence gives supporting details. This sentence gives more details. This sentence gives more details. This sentence gives more details. This sentence presents another supporting point. This sentence gives supporting details. This sentence gives more details. This sentence gives more details. This sentence gives more details. This sentence presents another supporting point. This sentence gives supporting details. This sentence gives more details. This sentence gives more details. This sentence gives more details. This sentence states the conclusion.

Example 2

This sentence states the main idea. This sentence presents a supporting point. This sentence gives supporting details. This sentence gives more details. This sentence gives more details. This sentence gives more details. This sentence gives more details.

This sentence presents another supporting point. This sentence gives supporting details. This sentence gives more details. This sentence gives more details. This sentence gives more details. This sentence gives more details. This sentence gives more details.

This sentence presents another supporting point. This sentence gives supporting details. This sentence gives more details. This sentence gives more details. This sentence gives more details. This sentence gives more details. This sentence states the conclusion.

PROCESS WRITING: AN OVERVIEW

When you write a composition, your goal is to communicate your ideas clearly to your audience (see *Note* below). In order to write clearly, you will need to complete certain steps in each stage of the process. In this process, you will

1. Write at least two drafts for each assignment. (Each time you write one version of a composition for one assignment, what you write is a "draft.")
2. Complete certain activities before and after each draft.

Note: "Audience" refers to the person or specific group of persons who will read your composition. In a classroom setting, this could be the instructor, your classmates, or a hypothetical group that your instructor selects. See Appendix 2, page 223.

The following gives the steps presented in this text.

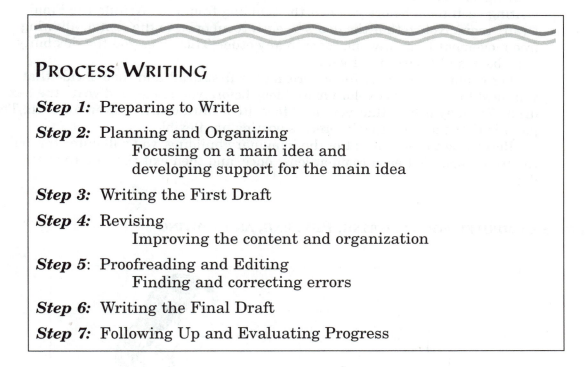

PROCESS WRITING

Step 1: Preparing to Write

Step 2: Planning and Organizing
Focusing on a main idea and
developing support for the main idea

Step 3: Writing the First Draft

Step 4: Revising
Improving the content and organization

Step 5: Proofreading and Editing
Finding and correcting errors

Step 6: Writing the Final Draft

Step 7: Following Up and Evaluating Progress

Following the process approach does not mean that you must follow the steps in order. Instead, process writing is flexible. In concept, process writing resembles the shape of an imaginary circular building with six rooms, as in this illustration.

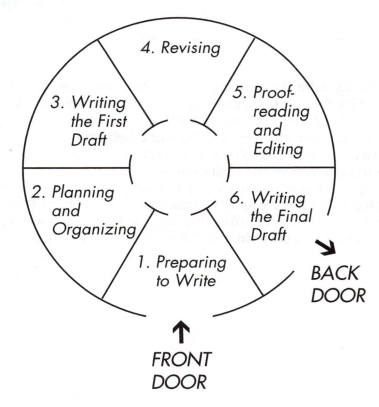

You enter through the front door into a room called "Preparing to Write." Leaving this first room, you move through the building, going to your left, visiting each room before you exit the building from the "Writing the Final Draft" room. Notice that the doors to each room open to the center, allowing free movement from any one room to any other. This gives you the flexibility to go back and revisit any room.

For example, you may finish writing the first draft and then decide that you need to go back to explore more ideas before you revise and write the next draft. You may decide that you need to write a third draft, or even a fourth. The point is that the activities in process writing are flexible.

Returning to the concept of the imaginary building, you will enter through the front door, visit each room at least once, and then exit through the back door.

USING A COMPUTER FOR DRAFTING, REVISING, AND EDITING

Writers used to claim that the eraser was their most useful tool. Now, however, with computers in so many homes and schools, the computer has become the writer's (and the student's) favorite tool.

Using a computer will save you time and help you produce higher-quality compositions. The reason is obvious: You can easily make changes on a draft without having to retype the entire paper.

When you first start using a computer for your writing assignments, you may feel that it is taking you extra time, because you have to get used to using a word processing program. After the first few times on the computer, though, you will find that you save time and even feel more creative.

SUGGESTIONS FOR USING THE COMPUTER

1. Accept the idea that you will need to spend a few sessions on the computer, before you become comfortable with it. Once you get past the initial discomfort, though, you will save time, produce higher-quality compositions, and enjoy the process more.

2. If your printer uses a ribbon, make sure that the ribbon is not worn out, and, if you have a choice, select a font that is easy to read.

3. If you use a spell-check program, evaluate the choices that the computer offers you very carefully. Remember that the computer does not offer suggestions based on the meaning of the word you are trying to spell. Instead, it simply gives you choices that contain similar letters to your misspelled word. You may still have to refer to a dictionary, but many word processing programs contain dictionaries for easy reference.

4. During your work session on the computer, save your material often on to the disk. Also, at the end of each session, print out a paper copy of your latest draft.

THREE ESSENTIALS FOR EFFECTIVE WRITING: A BIRD'S-EYE VIEW

Throughout this text, the following essentials are stressed, with greater focus on the first two. See Appendix 1, pages 220-222.

The First Essential: Clear, Convincing Content

- The composition meets the requirements of the assignment.

- The composition contains one clear main idea.

- The main idea is developed with plenty of specific supporting details.

The Second Essential: Clear Organization

- The first sentence states the main idea.*

- The middle sentences, called the body, develop and support the main idea with organized points and details.

- The last sentence, called the conclusion, ties the entire composition together and provides closure.

*Note: The main idea may appear at any position, or it even may be implied (not stated, but obvious). At this level of writing, however, you should put the main idea first.

```
┌─────────────────────────────────────────┐
│                  TITLE                    │
├─────────────────────────────────────────┤
│   ┌─────────────────────────────────┐    │
│   │          Main Idea              │    │
│   │                                 │    │
│   │                                 │    │
│   │            Body                 │    │
│   │                                 │    │
│   │                                 │    │
│   │         Conclusion              │    │
│   └─────────────────────────────────┘    │
│                                           │
└─────────────────────────────────────────┘
```

The Third Essential: Standard Grammar

- A final draft that uses standard grammar and is relatively free from any errors is an excellent goal for writers.

- Not all grammar points are equally important, however. See Appendix 4, page 235, and check with your instructor for the grammar points to focus on in your writing.

PARAGRAPH BASICS

A *paragraph* is a group of sentences about one main idea (or one point). It develops the main idea (or point) with specific supporting details.

The paragraph on the next page shows how a typical short composition appears on a sheet of notebook paper.

Teresa Poteranska
2/25/1997

My Sweet Grandmother

The most important person in my childhood was my grand-mother. I really loved going to her house during vacations. She would tell me fascinating stories about her life during World War II. Also, she would tell me fables, sometimes making up her own, with me as beautiful, magic princess. Often we went into the forest to pick raspberries and mushrooms. She taught me which ones to pick and which ones to avoid. When I was sad, my grandmother would rock me and sing to me. I can still hear her sweet and gentle voice. She died a few years ago, and I miss her very much.

PRACTICE A

Referring to the sample paragraph, answer the following questions.

1. What is the main idea in the sample paragraph?

_____

2. Where is the main idea located in the paragraph?

_____

3. Do the words in each line start at the far-left edge of the paper?

_____

4. Do the words in each line continue to the far-right edge of the paper?

_____

As you can see in the sample paragraph, open areas appear around the edges of the written material. These areas are called margins. (Notebook paper usually marks the left margin with a red margin line.)

Select A or B.

5. Does the first sentence start exactly at the far-left margin?

   A. Yes

   B. No

6. Where does the second sentence start?

   A. On the same line as the first sentence.

   B. On the line below the first sentence.

Note: In some cases, if a sentence ends at the right margin, the following sentence must start on the following line.

7. Where do all the rest of the sentences in the paragraph start in relationship to the sentences before them?

   A. If possible, on the same line as the previous sentence.

   B. Always on the line below the previous sentence.

BASIC GUIDELINES FOR PARAGRAPHS

1. The main idea of a paragraph appears in the first sentence.

   This guideline is recommended for developing writers. (Advanced writers might place the main idea in another position.)

2. Indent the first sentence of every new paragraph.

   The first sentence should start at approximately a half inch to the right of the red margin line.

3. Leave margins on the left and right edges.

   The left margin should start at the red line on your paper, and the right margin should leave a space of approximately a half inch between the written material and the right edge of your paper. This measurement will vary.

4. The sentences in a paragraph run continuously, with no breaks, from the first to the last sentence.

   After the first sentence, each sentence follows immediately after the previous sentence, if space allows.

5. Leave a space approximately the size of two letters between sentences.

   On a word processor, the size of this space will vary.

PRACTICE B

Which of the following (A or B) represents the correct format for a paragraph? Circle the title of your choice.

Choice A

Bla bla bla bla bla bla bla bla bla bla bla bla bla bla bla bla bla bla bla.
Bla bla bla bla bla bla bla bla bla bla bla bla.
Bla bla bla bla bla.
Bla Bla bla bla bla bla bla bla bla bla.

Choice B

    Bla bla bla bla bla bla bla bla bla. Bla bla bla bla. Bla bla bla bla bla bla bla bla bla bla. Bla bla bla bla bla bla bla bla. Bla bla bla bla bla bla bla bla bla.

PRACTICE C

Identify three problems in the following paragraph. You may refer to the Basic Guidelines for Paragraphs on the previous page. Write your answers in the spaces provided.

My Job Dissatisfaction

Lately, I have been unhappy with my job as a cashier at
McBuns.
First, the hours are a hardship for me.
I work from 3:00 to 11:00 in the evening, and I have trouble getting up
the next morning for class.
Next, the pay is miserable.I am making only twenty cents
above minimum wage.
Last, the people I work with are unfriendly.They never smile or want to
have a pleasant conversation.It is time to look for a new job.

---

1. _____

2. _____

3. _____

SAMPLE INSTRUCTOR'S MARKINGS TO CORRECT PARAGRAPH SHAPE

Your instructor may return your composition to you with markings to correct the paragraph format.

No two instructors mark compositions in exactly the same way, but your instructor might use these or similar markings on your paper.

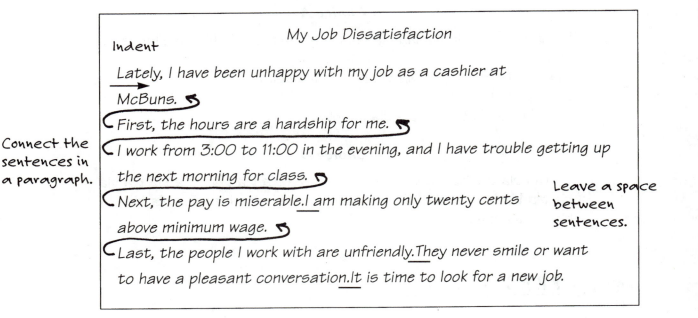

My Job Dissatisfaction

Indent

Lately, I have been unhappy with my job as a cashier at McBuns.

First, the hours are a hardship for me.

I work from 3:00 to 11:00 in the evening, and I have trouble getting up the next morning for class.

Next, the pay is miserable. I am making only twenty cents above minimum wage.

Last, the people I work with are unfriendly. They never smile or want to have a pleasant conversation. It is time to look for a new job.

Connect the sentences in a paragraph.

Leave a space between sentences.

 **PRACTICE**

Correct and rewrite the following paragraph. First, circle the sentence with the main idea and draw an arrow to move it to the beginning of the paragraph. Next, correct the format.

My Ideal Job

For one thing, the hours are great. I work weekend afternoons.

I love my job at Hank's Hot Dogs.

Next, the pay is okay for now. I make two dollars more than minimum wage.

Best of all, the people I work with are friendly. Two of my best friends work the same shift I do. I will probably keep this job for a few more years.

SECTION ONE

COMPOSING: THE BASICS

CHAPTER 1

Writing about a Person

For this chapter, you will interview one of your classmates and write a composition based on this interview. A successful composition presents your classmate as an individual with a unique personality.

Sample 1

Hope for the Future

Quang Ly is my new friend in my ESL writing class this semester. He   1
arrived here from Vietnam with his family almost a year ago. He is very
interested in engineering, and he dreams of being a successful engineer
in the future. He likes engineering because he enjoys fixing things. At home
he fixes whatever his family needs.

Quang spends his free time playing soccer or basketball with his friends.   2
Also, he likes the beach because it reminds him of his former
country, which he misses very much. When I asked about his childhood, a
serious look appeared on his face. He said that because of the war in
Indochina, fighting games with friends were popular. He did not say much

more about his memories of the war, but I felt that he had many kinds of experiences related to the war that have affected his life. He wants to go back to his country, but Vietnam is divided into two groups: those that support the communist government and those that want democracy.

I could really understand Quang's sadness about his country because my country Korea is in a similar situation. We talked about the future of our countries, and our hopes for them: the belief that one day our countries will be united in democracy. When that time comes, we both want to help to restore peace and harmony in our lands. Somehow, interviewing Quang gave me hope for the future of our two countries. 3

Adapted from a composition by Eunice Lee

What stands out for you about Quang?

_Vietnam, engineering, sad childhood b/c of ___ hope for future_
hopes peace + unific

Sample 2

My Courageous Classmate Seynab

Seynab Ahmad is one of my classmates in ESL 53A this semester. She is originally from Mogadishu, Somalia, and she came to this country two years ago. She lives with her sister now, and the rest of her family lives in San Diego. Seynab is attending school in order to become a doctor. 1

When I asked Seynab about her country, her eyes got wet, and then she told me her story. While she was at school in Somalia, fighting broke out between two enemy groups. When she ran back home, nobody was there, and she had no idea where her family had gone. Of course, she was terrified, so she fled. Three days later, she ended up in Marca, a small city in Somalia, where she found some people on their way to Kenya. Seynab did not speak the same language that these people did, but she escaped with them. Two years later she moved to London, where she found some relatives and learned that her family was in the United States. It took her three years to get a visa for the U.S., but she finally succeeded. She is very thankful now to be reunited with her family. 2

Seynab lived through many horrible experiences because of war and her separation from her family. I can understand how frightening it must be to escape alone and to try to adapt in a foreign country without any 3 support. This takes real courage. I really admire Seynab for her strength and for how she solved her problems, even though she was very young and without family to help her. I will always remember Seynab's courage.

Adapted from a composition by Syeda Rezvi

What stands out for you about Seynab?

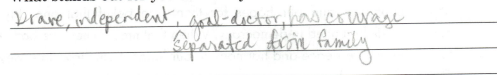

Brave, independent, goal-doctor, has courage
Separated from family

Sample 3

Thuy Pham: My Artistic Classmate

I met and interviewed Thuy Pham in my ESL writing class the second week of the semester. She is about twenty-five years old. She came to the United States from Vietnam with her family two years ago. Now she lives in Torrance with her parents and two brothers. To earn money, she does sewing at home, which she enjoys because she likes creating useful and attractive clothing. In order to get a better-paying job in the future, she is attending two ESL classes this semester. 1

Thuy likes the United States more than her home country because the living standard is higher here. For example, there are more opportunities for education, and transportation is easier. All in all, she feels more comfortable in this country. 2

In her free time, Thuy likes to watch TV, read novels in Vietnamese, design dresses, and visit with her friends. These four activities keep her satisfied. 3

From my conversations with Thuy, I concluded that she is artistic and a little introverted. She looked very serious when she was reading my first draft. After she finished reading, she asked me what the word "introverted" meant. I told her that it meant "quiet," and she nodded in agreement. When I asked her if she liked my first draft, she gave me a big smile. It felt wonderful to see Thuy's smile; it told me that she was happy and approved of what I had written about her. I am really glad I had the chance to talk with Thuy Pham. 4

Adapted from a composition by Hsi-Tai Chan

What stands out for you about Thuy? _____

_____

_____

_____

Sample 4

A New Friend with a Playful Sense of Humor

Victor Carrasco is in my ESL writing class this semester. He is 1
from Veracruz, Mexico, and he has been here for two years. His major is
electronics, and when I asked him why, he responded that he has always
enjoyed learning about how things work. When he was a child, he would
take radios and clocks apart, just to see how they worked. He added with
a smile, though, that his mother did not like his hobby.

Victor said he really likes this country. I asked him why, and he said that 2
it is easier to get an education here than it is in Mexico. At the time he
arrived, he could not speak English very well, so he had some trouble
communicating. Luckily, people were friendly, and he was able to learn
English at an adult school.

When I asked him what his dreams were for the future, he smiled, 3
pointed upwards, and said that he dreams of being up in the sky. His
answer surprised me. I did not understand what he meant, so I asked him
if he wanted to be in heaven. Then he laughed and said that he wanted to
fly in a jet to faraway countries, such as Spain and Japan to see how other
people live. His eyes sparkled when he spoke of traveling and
seeing other places.

Victor impressed me as a kind and funny guy. He told several jokes 4
during our interview, and I laughed a lot. With his friendly personality and
natural sense of humor, he will be successful in his new country and in his
travels to other places. I am glad to have a new friend like him.

Adapted from a composition by Takejiro Hirayama

What stands out for you about Victor?

_____

_____

_____

LOOKING AT CONTENT AND ORGANIZATION

The Main Idea

The first sentence of a paragraph usually states the *main idea*. For this interviewing assignment, a clear main idea includes the following:

The name of the interviewee: Quang Ly

Where and when you interviewed   in my ESL writing class this
the person: semester

> *Quang Ly is my new friend in my ESL writing class this semester.*

PRACTICE

Use the following information and write a sentence that states the main idea.

Who?   Ilya Glazunov
Where?   in Composition A
When?   last week

_____

_____

The Body

For this interviewing assignment, the *body* of the composition contains the following types of support:

1. Basic background information about the interviewee, such as country of origin, family information, and educational goals:

> *He arrived here from Vietnam with his family almost a year ago. He is very interested in engineering, and he dreams of being a successful engineer in the future.*

2. Personal information about the interviewee, such as interests and opinions:

> *Quang spends his free time playing soccer or basketball with his friends. Also, he likes the beach because it reminds him of his former country, which he misses very much.*

3. The writer's personal reaction to the interview:

AT

I could really understand Quang's sadness about his country because my country Korea is in a similar situation.

PRACTICE A

The following sentences are from the sample compositions. Identify the type of information for each sentence. Write B, P, or W on the line.

B = Basic background information about the interviewee
P = Personal information about the interviewee, such as interests and opinions
W = The writer's personal reaction to the interview

__P__ 1. Thuy likes the United States more than her home country because the living standard is higher here.

_____ 2. She is originally from Mogadishu, Somalia, and she came to this country two years ago.

_____ 3. It felt wonderful to see Thuy's smile; it told me that she was happy and approved of what I had written about her.

_____ 4. With his friendly personality and natural sense of humor, he will have a lot of success in his new country and in his travels to other places.

_____ 5. He is very interested in engineering, and he dreams of being a successful engineer in the future.

_____ 6. I can understand how frightening it must be to escape alone and to try to adapt in a foreign country without any support.

_____ 7. To earn money, she does sewing at home, which she enjoys because she likes creating useful and attractive clothing.

_____ 8. When I asked him what his dreams were for the future, he smiled, pointed upwards, and said that he dreams of being up in the sky.

_____ 9. Victor impressed me as a kind and funny guy. He told several jokes during our interview, and I laughed a lot.

Using your imagination, write one or two sentences for each of the three types of information to support the following main idea:

> I met and interviewed Ilya Glazunov in my Composition A class last week.

1. Basic background information about the interviewee:
   (*Hint*: The name is Russian.)

   Ilya is from _____

   _____

   _____

   _____

   _____

2. Personal information about the interviewee, such as interests and opinions:

   _____

   _____

   _____

   _____

   _____

   _____

3. The writer's personal reaction to the interview:

   _____

   _____

   _____

   _____

   _____

The Conclusion

The *conclusion*, usually the last sentence, ties together the entire composition. Often it gives the writer's strongest impression of the interview.

> Somehow, interviewing Quang gave me hope for the future of our two countries.

PRACTICE A

In the following pairs of sentences, one sentence is a conclusion, and one is not. Circle the letter of the conclusion.

1. **(A.)** I will always remember Seynab's courage.
   B. She is very thankful to be reunited with her family.

2. A. I met and interviewed Thuy Pham in my ESL writing class the second week of the semester.
   B. I am really glad I had the chance to talk with Thuy Pham.

3. A. I am glad to have a new friend like him.
   B. His eyes sparkled when he spoke of traveling and seeing other countries.

PRACTICE B

Write a conclusion for the composition about Ilya Glazunov from Practice B on the opposite page.

_____

_____

PRACTICING WHAT YOU HAVE LEARNED

The following is a list of notes Sandra took during her interview of Faiza Fazeli. (Interview notes don't have to be written in complete sentences.) Identify the types of information for each entry. Write the letter of the correct answer.

M = Main idea information
B = Basic background information about the interviewee
P = Personal information such as interests and opinions
W = The writer's reaction
C = Conclusion

<u>P</u>   1. Loves dancing

_____   2. Met in reading and writing class this semester

_____ 3. I enjoyed talking to Faiza about dancing because my hobby is dancing, too.

_____ 4. Immigrated to this country two years ago

_____ 5. Thinks that English speakers talk too fast and use too many idiomatic expressions

_____ 6. Wants to be a dentist

_____ 7. Does not like the way some people in this country fear the Muslim religion

_____ 8. She thinks that some people believe that most Muslims are extremists, but this isn't true!

_____ 9. I learned a lot about her religion.

_____ 10. Wishes non-Muslims understood her religion better

_____ 11. I enjoyed interviewing Faiza and hope we can learn more about each other in the future.

_____ 12. Lives with her parents and brother

YOUR TURN TO WRITE

Step 1: Preparing to Write

DETERMINING YOUR AUDIENCE

Before you start any writing assignment, you need to identify your audience. Knowing your audience will help you write appropriately for that specific person or group.

For this assignment, is your instructor the only person who will read your composition? Will other students in your class read it? If your audience is your classmates, your instructor might want you to write in an informal style.

If you have any doubts about your audience, check with your instructor. See Appendix 2, page 223.

SELECTING AN INTERVIEW PARTNER

Your instructor will guide you in selecting an interview partner. Your partner should be someone you do not already know.

EXPLORING IDEAS

Listing Ideas. Write a list of questions to ask your interview partner. These questions will help you get started in your interview. Some topics you may want to ask about include the following:

Basic Background Information

Place of birth
Moving to a new place to live
Family
Goals or plans for the future

Interests and Opinions

Hobbies and pastimes
Opinions about this school/city/country
Surprising or funny experiences in a new situation, such as at
    a new school or on a vacation
Opinions about current events
Things your partner has a strong opinion about: family, friendships,
    politics, religion, health, success, and so forth
Self-description (personality)
Other (your idea): _____

Interviewing. With your partner, take turns interviewing each other. You are not limited to the questions on your list. Instead, you are free to explore any topic that you and your partner find interesting.

Take notes. You will refer to them when you write your composition. See Appendix 2, page 224.

Step 2: *Planning and Organizing*

Before you write your first draft, you need to plan ahead and organize your ideas.

Some experienced writers can organize their ideas in their heads. Others prefer organizing their ideas on paper. For you, as a developing writer, it may be helpful to organize your ideas on paper. See Appendix, 2 page 226.

MAKING A ROUGH OUTLINE

One common method to organize ideas is to make a rough outline. Many student writers find this technique the easiest and most effective way. Leave out any ideas that do not contribute to an effective composition. Use the outline format on the next page as a guide.

OUTLINE

Main idea

    Who? _____

    Where? _____

    When? _____

Body
    Basic background
    information _____

    _____

    _____

    Personal information
    (interests and
    opinions) _____

    _____

    _____

    _____

    Writer's reactions _____

    _____

    _____

Conclusion _____

    _____

    _____

Here is a sample outline with key words and phrases:

OUTLINE

Main idea

    Who?   *Faiza Fazeli*

    Where?   *Writing class*

    When?   *this semester*

Body
Basic background information

     came here 2 years ago with parents and brother

     wants to be a dentist

Personal information (interests and opinions)

     Eng. speakers talk too fast

     loves to dance

     some people fear her religion

     have wrong ideas

     wishes people understood

Writer's reactions   *dancing, my hobby, too*

     religion, I learned a lot

Conclusion   *enjoyed it*

     want to learn more in future

Step 3: Writing the First Draft

Using your notes and outline, write your first draft. Focus on content and organization, and worry about grammar later — in the second or final draft.

As you write your draft you may discover that you want to get more information from your partner. If so, ask your partner additional questions. See Appendix 2, page 227.

Step 4: Revising

Revising means improving the content and organization of your draft. When you revise, you can add material, eliminate material, or move material from one spot to another. Use any system you wish to make your revisions clear to yourself. The following example shows possible revisions for a typical first draft. See Appendix 2, page 227.

My Classmate Gloria Figueroa

Gloria Figueroa is in my ESL writing class with me this semester. I hope we will become good friends. She came from El Salvador five years ago.

Gloria enjoys living in this country because she has more freedom here than she had in her country. *Add details.* In her free time, Gloria likes to visit the Hawthorne Plaza with friends. *Add details.* Maybe some day she will return to El Salvador to visit her family, but she wants to make this country her new home.

Gloria is a very friendly and outgoing person. She smiles and laughs a lot. Her friendliness put me at ease right away. We had a lot of fun together.

Adapted from a composition by Chamroeun Thong

Discussion

"I hope we will become good friends" is moved to the end because it's a general statement that points to the future and gives closure.

"Maybe some day she will return to El Salvador . . . .*" is moved to the position after ". . . El Salvador five years ago" because it discusses the same ideas: El Salvador and her home.

More details are needed after ". . . more freedom than she had in her country" because the reader will want to know specifically what Gloria means by "more freedom." Possible details: For example, she can go anywhere she wants to, such as to the beach, the malls, or the movies.

More details are also needed after ". . . to visit the Hawthorne Plaza with friends" because the reader will be curious about what Gloria does there. Possible details: to window shop, try clothes on, eat fries at Burger King, and laugh and talk with her friends.

* Ellipses consist of three dots (. . .). They mark where a section is deleted from quoted material.

 **PRACTICE**

Revise the following draft. Circle two sentences that need to be moved, and draw arrows to indicate where they should be moved. Add details after the second sentence. In addition, cross out any words or sentences that are not necessary.

My Classmate Maria Espinoza

I met and interviewed Maria Espinoza in my ESL writing class in spring, 1997, of this year. Maria likes living in the United States because she likes the political system and other things about this country. Also, I think she likes being near her grandchildren so that she can watch them grow up. One of her grandchildren goes to nursery school. She came from Cuba nine years ago to join her son and his family. One thing she does not like about this country is the attitude of the teenagers. She says that teenagers do not respect their parents enough, and she hopes that her grandchildren will grow up with good, old-fashioned family values.

1

I really enjoyed interviewing Maria. I appreciate Maria's concern. I have heard my own parents state similar opinions, but I am certain that with Maria's love and guidance, her grandchildren will grow up with strong family values.

2

Review your draft for ways to revise it. You may do this by peer response and/or self-evaluation.

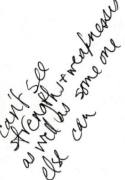

can't see strength + weakness as will as some one else can

PEER RESPONSE

Peer response serves two important purposes. First, it gives you valuable practice in analyzing a draft for improvement. Second, it gives you useful input from your partner to help you to revise your own draft. See Appendix 2, page 227.

Exchange drafts with your partner. Follow these general guidelines:

1. Read your partner's draft twice. The second time you read it, discuss any unclear spots with your partner.
2. Check the draft for clear organization. Refer to Checkpoints for Revision, which follows. Point out any possible problems to your partner.
3. Ask your partner further interview questions for additional details for your composition.

Note: You and your partner must make the final decisions about what to change (or not to change) in your own compositions.

SELF-EVALUATION

Analyze your own draft for ways to improve the content and organization. The best way to do this is to set your draft aside for at least twenty-four hours so that you can evaluate it with a fresh mind. Refer to Checkpoints for Revision given here.

✔ CHECKPOINTS FOR REVISION

Overall Organization

- Are the ideas organized according to the outline in Step 2?

Other

- Does the composition present the interviewee as an interesting and unique individual?

Step 5: Proofreading and Editing

Proofreading means looking for errors. *Editing* means correcting the errors. (Some people use these two terms interchangeably.)

In this step, you will proofread and edit your draft for grammatical errors and visual presentation.

When you edit, you can

- Cross out any words or letters you want to eliminate.
- Use a caret (^) to add material above the caret.
- Correct any other errors.

Example

> My Classmate Maria Espinoza
>
> I met and interviewed Maria Espinoza in my
> ESL wri~~t~~ting class in spring, 1997. She ~~comes~~ ^came^
> from Cuba nine year^s^ ago to join ^her^ son and
> his family.

PRACTICE

Proofread and edit the following draft. Find these errors.

	Number of Errors to Find
Spelling	3
Missing subject	2
Missing verb	1
Run-on sentence	1
Sentence fragment	2
Present or past tense	3

My Classmate Maria Espinoza

I met and interviewed Maria Espinoza in my ESL writting class.   1

In spring, 1997. She comes from Cuba nine years ago to join her son

and his family.   3

Maria likes living in United States becaus likes the political system better here. She prefers democracy over communism. Also, 5

she like being near her grandchildren. So that she can watch

them grow up. One thing she does not like about this country is the 7

attitude of the teenagers. Says that teenagers do not respect

their parents enough, and she hopes that her grandchildren grow 9

up with good, old-fashioned family values.

I appreciate Maria's concern, I have heard my own parents 11

state a similer opinion. But I certain that with Maria's love and

guidance, her grandchildren will grow up with strong family values. 13

I really enjoy interviewing Maria.

YOUR TURN

Proofread and edit your draft for grammar and visual presentation. You may do this by peer response and/or self-evaluation.

PEER RESPONSE

This activity gives you valuable practice in proofreading. It also gives you useful input from your partner that will help you edit your own draft.

Exchange drafts with your partner. Read your partner's draft twice. The second time you read it, point out possible errors to him or her. Refer to the Checkpoints for Proofreading and Editing that follows.

Of course, you and your partner must make the final decisions about what to change (or not to change) in your own composition.

SELF-EVALUATION

Proofread and edit your own draft. The best way to do this is to set your draft aside for at least twenty-four hours so that you can evaluate it with a fresh mind. See Appendix 2, page 228. Refer to Checkpoints for Proofreading and Editing on the opposite page.

Step 6: Writing the Final Draft

Write your final draft with the revisions and corrections. After you finish, proofread and edit it again carefully. See Appendix 2, page 229.

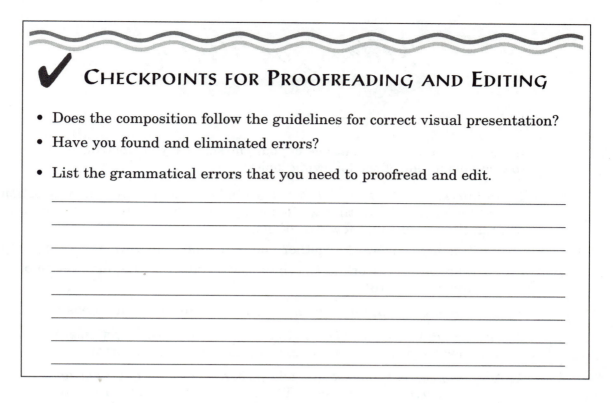

✔ CHECKPOINTS FOR PROOFREADING AND EDITING

- Does the composition follow the guidelines for correct visual presentation?
- Have you found and eliminated errors?
- List the grammatical errors that you need to proofread and edit.

_____

_____

_____

_____

_____

_____

_____

_____

Note: Some instructors combine both revising and editing in the same peer-response activity. Other instructors limit peer response to revising only. Make sure you understand which method your instructor prefers.

Step 7: *Following Up and Evaluating Progress*

SHARING YOUR WRITING WITH OTHERS

Small-Group Response. You will do this activity before you turn in your final draft to the instructor. Follow these steps:

1. Form a small group of approximately four students.
2. Exchange compositions and read each others' compositions.
3. As a group, decide which of the compositions is the most convincing or enjoyable. Do not comment on the organization or the grammar. Do not say anything negative.
4. Draw a small star in the upper left-hand corner of the composition that your group selected, and be prepared to discuss the reasons your group selected this composition.

BENEFITING FROM FEEDBACK

After your instructor returns your composition to you, make sure you understand your patterns of strengths and weaknesses. Then, in the future, you can focus on building on your strengths and eliminating your weaknesses. See Appendix 2, page 231.

Ideas for Writing

In addition to writing about one of your classmates, your instructor may ask you to write about one of the following topics:

1. *An interview with the instructor.* The students ask the instructor questions and take notes. Next, they write a composition based on the information from the instructor. A few variations:

   a. Small groups work together and write one composition in each group.

   b. Small groups work at the chalkboard and write the composition on the chalkboard.

2. *A group or class interview with one student.* (See above for ideas.)

3. *An interview with an older relative.* Examples of people you might interview: a grandparent, an aunt, or an uncle, and so forth.

4. *A topic of current interest that will form the basis for questions for interviews with several people.* The interviewees can be classmates or people outside of class. Limit the topic to a few questions, and report on your findings in your composition.

5. *A topic of interest related to a specific group of people.* Examples of people you might interview:

   a. Single mothers   What kinds of special challenges do they face?

   b. ESL students who are ready to graduate from your school   What factors helped them be successful in school?

   c. People married for more than ten years   What qualities contribute to a successful marriage?

6. *Your own idea.* Do you have an idea for a composition about a person? If so, present the idea to your instructor who will determine if your idea is appropriate for this assignment.

   Important: You need the instructor's approval before you start the assignment.

CHAPTER 2

Narrating
a Personal Experience

In this chapter, you will write about a personal experience that affected you in some way.

This experience will consist of a single event that took place during a short period of time — perhaps a few days, a few hours, or even less. You will express your dominant (strongest) emotion or opinion about the event, and you will explain what happened, with moment-to-moment details to recreate the experience and support your emotion or opinion.

Have you ever visited a place of great beauty?

Sample 1

Climbing Mount Kyaik-tiyo

When my family and I climbed Mount Kyaik-tiyo to see one of the most admirable Buddhist pagodas in Myanmar, the former Burma, I discovered total peace. On the way up, we passed small souvenir shops and monasteries. We met other people who were climbing at the same time, and we enjoyed the pleasant conversation. We passed waterfalls and watched monkeys playing in the trees. After sunset, we used a torch to light the way through the stillness. When we arrived at the top, we were tired, but happy, because the gentle music from the pagoda gave us new strength and serenity.   1

Early the next morning, everyone entered the pagoda to worship. Some people poured water on the statue of Buddha to wash away their sins. Others meditated. Visitors decorated the pagoda with candles and beautiful fresh flowers. Everyone's face reflected the harmony and tranquility all around us. After I worshiped, I looked around and saw the huge green mountains surrounding me. The splendor of both the pagoda and nature brought complete peace to my mind.   2

That evening we returned down the mountain. As we descended, we reminded each other of the beauty and peace we had experienced. I want to keep this peace in my heart forever.   3

Adapted from a composition by Mar (Ni Ni) Lay

What is Ni Ni's emotion or opinion about her experience?

_____

_____

_____

Have you ever had an embarrassing situation at a restaurant?

Sample 2

The Fugitive

About two years ago I had an embarrassing incident when my family 1
and I went out to a Korean barbecue restaurant. The food and service were
excellent, and we had a great time. While we were relaxing after dinner, my
mom got change for the tip. Then we paid our bill and left.

On our way to the car, we talked about how good the restaurant was, 2
and how we should come back here again. When I got into the car, I made
my belt loose so that I could sit comfortably. I started to drive away when the
headwaiter approached the car and asked, "Was anything wrong
with our service?" "No, no!" I told him. "Everything was terrific! Why do you
ask?" "You didn't leave any tip," he explained. I paused for a second and
then looked at my mom and asked, "Mom, did you leave the tip?" With
a puzzled look on her face she said, "I think I did. No, maybe I
didn't. I don't know!" Then I said to her, "Check your pocket. Maybe you
didn't leave it on the table." When she reached into her pocket, she found
the tip. "Oh, I'm so sorry," she said with an embarrassed look on her
face. I was ashamed, too, because I felt like a fugitive. Immediately, I
apologized to the headwaiter and handed him the tip. Now we always
double-check to make sure that we leave a tip for the waiters.

Adapted from a composition by Masaki Takada

What is Masaki's emotion or opinion about his experience?

_____

_____

_____

Have you ever panicked on a trip because you forgot to pack something important?

Sample 3

A Minor Panic

All because of a minor detail, I panicked during my airplane trip to the 1
United States. Everything started like a wonderful dream. It was my first time
on an airplane, and I was excited about touching the ground of the United
States later that day.

As we took off from the Samoan airport for Hawaii, everyone got an 2
immigration form to fill out. The form asked for the address where I would be

staying in the United States. I did not bring the address with me because I thought all I needed was the phone number. I kept staring at the form. Eventually, I panicked because I thought immigration would give me a lot of trouble if I didn't have the address. I could not calm down and I was nervous during the entire flight.

When I got to Hawaii, the immigration officer smiled at me right away. His smile made me think of the Tongan proverb "It is like pouring oil on a rough sea," and this gave me hope that he would help me solve my problem. He suggested that I use the address of the college I was going to attend. Thus, the problem was easily solved. On the flight from Hawaii to the mainland, I had to laugh at myself for getting so panicky over such a minor detail.
3

Adapted from a composition by Lomio Fuahala

What is Lomio's emotion or opinion about his experience?

_____

_____

_____

Have you ever been robbed?

Sample 4

Welcome to the Big City

I had the most terrifying experience of my life two years ago when I was a newcomer to the city. I was working as a delivery man for Domino's Pizza, and I had to make a night delivery. The neighborhood I went to looked abandoned and isolated, with almost no lights on at all. After I delivered the pizza, I was heading back to my car with the money in my hand. When I stepped out of the apartment building, a tall man suddenly blocked my way and tried to grab the money, saying with a rough voice, "Give me the money, or you're dead!" By instinct or reflex, I stepped back, but then I felt someone grabbing me from behind around my neck and putting a gun to my head. I was trapped. The first guy threatened me again and kept demanding the money. However, I couldn't talk because his partner was squeezing my throat. From the corner of my eye I could also see the muzzle of the gun just one inch from my head. I was petrified. I knew that they could easily kill me.
1

Of course, they took the money — about fifty-five dollars. Before they left, however, they pushed me down on the pavement and kicked me hard several times. Somehow, I made it back to my car and drove away.
2

The fear from that night will always remain with me, but the experience   3
taught me how to handle this kind of situation. The key is to keep cool and
be cooperative.

Adapted from a composition by Esteban Andiola

What is Esteban's emotion or opinion about his experience?

_____

_____

_____

Have native English speakers ever misunderstood you when you were speaking
in English?

Sample 5

A Misunderstanding

Last spring semester my difficulty pronouncing the "f," "p," and "r"   1
sounds got me into trouble with the El Camino College police. One day I
was running late for my math class. To make things worse, I could not find a
parking place. I did not want to be too late or miss class altogether, so I
parked in a spot marked for visitors. After class I went back to my car and
found a parking ticket on the windshield. This was the first ticket I'd ever
gotten in my life, so I was very upset. Immediately, I rushed to the campus
police department.

When a young lady came to the window to help me, I told her, "I got   2
a parking ticket. What can I do?" At least, that's what I thought I had said but
all the people in the room stared at me with a startled look. Shocked, the
young woman asked, "What did you say?" My first thought was that she
had not heard me because my voice was too soft, so I repeated in a louder,
huskier voice, "I got a parking ticket, and I want to do something about it!"
There was a long silence before everybody in the room burst out laughing.

The incident felt like a nightmare at the time, but now I can laugh about   3
it. Since then, I have learned to pronounce the "f" and "p" sounds more
distinctly. I can also pronounce the "r" sound more clearly.

Adapted from a composition by Lawrence Han

What is Lawrence's emotion or opinion about his experience?

_____

_____

_____

What's Your Opinion?

Read the sample compositions again, and select the composition you think is the most effective and enjoyable to read. With your classmates, discuss your choice and the reasons for it. You may use any of the following reasons, or write additional ones.

1. The humor is enjoyable.
2. The entire narration is convincing. The writer helps me feel the emotion or opinion.
3. The narration is original, or the writer tells it in an original way.
4. The tone is honest and sincere.
5. I have had a similar personal experience.
6. I am interested in what the writer learned.

   Additional reasons:

7. _____

8. _____

Your choice: _____

Your reasons: _____

LOOKING AT CONTENT AND ORGANIZATION

The Main Idea

A clear main idea includes a *topic* and a *comment*. The topic is the writer's experience. The comment is the writer's opinion, emotion, or other idea about the experience.

The experience:	
When?	about two years ago
Who?	my family and I
What/Where?	dinner at a Korean barbecue restaurant
Comment:	embarrassment

About two years ago I had an embarrassing incident when my family and I went out to a Korean barbecue restaurant.

 **PRACTICE A**

Read the following narration. In the main idea, underline the topic once and the comment twice. In addition, circle all the words in the body and the conclusion that remind you of the main idea.

A Decision and the Courage to Carry It Out

After a lot of hesitation, I developed the courage to register for English 1
classes last year. At first, I did not feel confident about talking to people in
order to register, but I knew that I needed to improve my English to get a job.

When I arrived at the school, I did not go in. I just stood at the door 2
for a while and then returned home. On the way home, many discussions took
place in my mind. I stood on the line between fear and hope.

Two days later, I decided to go back to the school to register. I was 3
scared, but this time I went inside the building. After standing silently near
the door for a long time, I went outside again because I still didn't have
enough courage to talk to anyone. When I was outside again, though, I
made up my mind to go back inside.

People came, registered, and left while I sat quietly. Finally, a clerk turned 4
to me and asked me, "May I help you, sir?" My heart was thumping, but I
stood up and told him that I wanted to register. I used my best English and
registered for a class.

On the way home, I was smiling and I was very proud of myself for 5
making a decision and finding the courage to carry it out.

Adapted from a composition by Vu Dang

 **PRACTICE B**

*Circle the letter of what you think is the best main idea in each of the following groups.
Compare your answers with your classmates, and discuss the reasons for your choices.*

1. A. It took me two frustrating years to learn how to drive a stick shift.

   B. The first time I tried driving a stick shift was one of the most
frustrating days of my life.

   C. I learned how to drive with a stick shift shortly after I moved to
this city.

2. A. I had an exhausting but thrilling time hiking to the bottom of the
Grand Canyon last summer.

   B. Last year when I visited the Grand Canyon, I hiked to the bottom.

   C. Hiking to the bottom of Grand Canyon last year was more exhausting
than it was worth. *the*

3. A. My first attempt at wallpapering turned out to be disastrous.

   B. One day last spring my husband and I wallpapered the baby's room.

   C. I've wallpapered three rooms in my house over the past year, and I've
hated every minute of it.

4. A. In my first week in this country, I was embarrassed over a silly mistake I made while I was shopping for a birthday present at the Del Amo Mall.

   B. I hate embarrassing situations.

   C. In my first week in this country, I had a wonderful time shopping at the Del Amo Mall; but my fun was spoiled when I made a silly mistake.

5. A. Last Monday evening, while I was watching TV, the telephone rang.

   B. Last Monday evening, while I was watching TV, I got a phone call that made me angry.

   C. Last Monday evening, while I was watching TV, the telephone rang, and a strange voice asked me, "Are you the lady of the house?"

The Body

BACKGROUND INFORMATION

You may need to start some narrations with brief background information. This background information sets the stage for the action.

In the following example, the background information is underlined.

The first time I went hunting with my uncle I was scared to death. I was only nine years old when Uncle Joe convinced my mother that I was old enough for a deer hunting adventure in the Vancouver wilderness.

 **PRACTICE**

Underline the background information in the following student composition.

A Disappointment in My Brother

Last summer I was very disappointed with my younger brother's bad judgment. My brother had come from Austria to visit us on his vacation. One day he was in the backyard playing with our younger nephew. They went into the storage shed. I could see them from my bedroom. When they did not come out for a long time, I got curious and decided to see what they were doing. What I saw was a horror! In the middle of the shed was a fire. They were burning small cars and gum. When I saw the fire, I was furious! I was so disappointed in my brother because he was eighteen years old and should have known better than to show fire to a small kid. From then on, it was hard to trust my brother again.

Adapted from a composition by Teresa Poteranska

Is the background information longer or shorter than the action that follows it? _____

THE ACTION

The body relates the action, using specific details to make the action come alive for the reader. These details support the main idea and help the reader picture the action, moment by moment, as in the following excerpt from Esteban's composition.

> ... When I stepped out of the apartment building, a tall man suddenly 1
> blocked my way and tried to grab the money, saying with a rough voice,
> "Give me the money, or you're dead!" By instinct or reflex, I stepped back,
> but then I felt someone grabbing me from behind around my neck and
> putting a gun to my head. I was trapped. The first guy threatened me again
> and kept demanding the money. However, I couldn't talk because his
> partner was squeezing my throat. From the corner of my eye I could also
> see the muzzle of the gun just one inch from my head. I was petrified. I
> knew that they could easily kill me.
>
> Of course, they took the money — about fifty-five dollars. Before they 2
> left, however, they pushed me down on the pavement and kicked me hard
> several times. Somehow, I made it back to my car and drove away.

Is this excerpt convincing? Why or why not?

_____

_____

_____

 **PRACTICE**

Identify the sentence in each pair that describes action more clearly or gives better details. Circle the letter of your answer. Then, working with your classmates, identify the words in each answer that make the sentence clearer and better detailed.

Stuck in the Mud

On the way from the Grand Canyon to Phoenix, Arizona, two years ago, my husband and I had a wonderful experience when we got stuck in the mud. This may sound strange, but let me tell you my story. We decided to take a shortcut on a dirt road. We saw some black clouds forming ahead, but we did not think much about them. We didn't realize that we were heading for trouble.

1. (A.) Within ten minutes, it started to rain hard, with wild winds.
   B. Soon the weather turned very bad, and there was rain.

2. A. Huge amounts of dirty water turned the road into a river, and we got stuck in the soft mud.
   B. Lots of water came down, there was water everywhere, and we could not drive any further.

3. A. We struggled to get out for a long time, but nothing happened no matter what we did.
   B. We struggled to get out for six hours with no success, and nobody passed by.

4. A. When it started to get dark, we became desperate and soon afterwards lost hope.
   B. When it started to get dark, we felt very bad, and later we felt even worse.

5. A. Then we saw evidence of people somewhere in the distance.
   B. Then we saw some smoke coming from the other side of the hill.

6. A. With new hope, we climbed up over the muddy hill and met a young couple.
   B. Feeling better, we went to look for the people and met a young couple.

7. A. Luckily, they had a four-wheel drive car, and they pulled our car out of the mud.
   B. Luckily, they had the necessary equipment, and they did us a big favor and helped us.

8. A. After that, they were very kind and offered to help us in any way they could.
   B. After that, they offered to accompany us until we reached the paved road.

9. A. We had several more problems along the way, but each time we needed assistance, they helped us.
   B. We got stuck again many times along the way, but each time they pulled us out.

10. A. I was happy when our terrible experience was finally over.
    B. I was happy when I finally saw the lights of civilization.

Thanks to the kindness of this couple, our vacation ended happily. Since then, we have corresponded with them and developed a wonderful friendship.

Adapted from a composition by Teruyo Tsuchiya

The Conclusion

The conclusion of your composition ties together the entire piece. It may contain one or more of the following:

- A restatement of the main idea in another way
- A related thought that grows out of the body, such as the significance of the experience for you; that is, what you learned or how you changed
- A look to the future

Which of the above conclusion types appears in the following student composition?

The Most Terrifying Day of My Life

The most terrifying day of my life started when my daughter had a terrible accident with hot cooking oil. It was on June 17, 1991. I had gone to school to register for classes. By the time I got home, I was very hungry and tired. I started preparing some enchiladas, and just when the oil had gotten hot, my daughter came to ask me for water. As I turned to give her the water, I bumped the handle of the pan, spilling the hot oil all over her legs. I still remember her terrible screaming from the pain. I looked at her legs, and the skin looked like hot melted wax. In horror, I rushed her to the hospital. 1

At the hospital, a doctor treated her burns, while I walked back and forth in the waiting room, crying and praying. To make matters worse, though, an administrator at the hospital accused me of child abuse. She refused to believe that it was an accident. This only added to my anguish. 2

My daughter and I did not get home until the next day after the social worker had cleared me. Although I was finally able to go home with my daughter, the scars on her legs will always remind me of that terrible day. 3

Adapted from a composition by Gema Martinez

What makes Gema's composition successful?

_____

_____

_____

PRACTICE

Go back to the sample compositions at the beginning of this chapter. For each composition, identify the conclusion. Next, with your classmates, discuss the effectiveness of each conclusion. Finally, using various ways to write conclusions, rewrite each ending.

LANGUAGE TIPS

Past Time

Most narrations contain a lot of action verbs. Also, because a narration relates an event from the past, most verbs appear in one of the past time verb forms: simple past, past progressive, or other verbs referring to past time.

Most of the verbs in the following example appear in one of the past tense forms.

The Terror of War

The most frightening hour of my life **took** place during the war between Iran and Iraq. Because I **was** ill, I **had** to have emergency surgery. The day after the operation, I **was** weak and unable to move. It **was** early in the evening, and my mother **was visiting** me. Suddenly I **heard** the sound of a siren, and shortly after that, I **heard** the sounds of patients screaming and running for shelter. I **was** terrified. I **begged** my mother to go and find shelter, but she **refused** and **said**, "I will never leave you alone!" Enemy jets **were attacking** the city with rockets, and the windows **were breaking** from the force of the explosions. The lights **went** out, and I **could** not **see** anything. I just **listened** to the voices of the patients nearby screaming. After the war planes **left**, the nurses **started** assisting those who **could** not **move** by themselves. They **took** us to another room on the other side of the hospital away from the rocket damage. We **prayed** that the planes **would** not return. I doubt that I will ever forget the terrible fear I **experienced** that evening.

Adapted from a composition by Farnaz Dastmalchi

1. Is Farnaz's composition convincing? Why or why not?

_____

2. Which sentence(s) made the strongest impression on you? Write the verb(s).

_____

Direct Quotations

Direct quotations include the exact words that someone spoke or wrote. These exact words provide specific supporting details that help the action come alive. The following student composition contains several examples of direct quotations.

Doing My Best

I felt proud when my team came in second in a four-hundred-meter relay race in high school. My team had four runners. We had practiced a lot for the race, and we easily won the preliminary matches.   1

When the final event began, I felt scared. What if I fell down? If I did, would we lose? My coach patted my shoulder and said, "Have confidence. You will do well." I glanced at the other runners. They looked full of confidence. My heart was pounding, and my legs were shaking. "Bang!" As soon as the gun sounded, I started to run, but I slipped and fell, just as I had worried. My coach shouted, "Jiwon! Run!" I stood up and started to run again. "We are going to lose because of me," I thought, but I did not give up. I just did my best. The crowd was cheering, and the race was over soon. We finished in second place. "Good job! You guys did your best!" our coach told us.   2

I have not run since I graduated from high school. I would like to run again, but more than this, I want to feel the pride of doing my best again.   3

Adapted from a composition by Jiwon Kim

1. Which quotation was the most effective in drawing you into Jiwon's experience? _____
   _____
   _____

2. Why? _____
   _____
   _____

Edit the following composition by correcting any verb errors and by adding quotation marks where necessary.

A Mistake at the Library

One year ago I had an embarrassing situation at the Irvine library. I sat   1

studied

at my favorite table and ~~study~~ for a while. About one hour later, I start to

feel a little hungry, so I left for a snack.   3

When I come back to my table, I was surprised. I see a beautiful young

girl sitting in my chair, reading my book, and putting my book bag under   5

the table. I walk over to her and said, Would you like to borrow my book?

She just stared at me and smile strangely. I repeated my question, and she   7

laugh. I think you made a mistake, she said. I am confused and did not

know what to think at first. She continued, I saw you sitting over there a   9

while ago, and she points to a table about five tables away from where

we were. I really felt embarrassed when I realize that I had made such a   11

ridiculous mistake. I just said, Sorry! And I hurry back to my table. Now that

I look back on this situation, I don't feel so embarrassed about it   13

anymore, but I sure feel embarrassed at the time.

Adapted from a composition by Hai Tran

1. What makes Hai's composition successful?

_____

_____

_____

2. Have you had any similar experiences? Explain.

_____

_____

_____

PRACTICING WHAT YOU HAVE LEARNED

Put the sentences in the following narration in order. Underline the information in each sentence that helps you identify its order.

My First and Last Camping Trip

I had a frightening experience on a camping trip in Armenia a year ago. My family wanted to go camping. I was afraid of the idea of sleeping outdoors in a tent in the mountains, but I made up my mind to go anyway.

A. _____ When I looked through the keyhole, I saw a big brown bear near the rest rooms, where the trash cans were.

B. _____ When I got to the rest room, I heard sounds coming from the woods.

C. _1_ When we got to the campsite, the ranger told us to be careful of the bears that come out of the woods at night.

D. _____ I had a great time, until the third night.

E. _____ I remembered what the ranger said about the bears coming out only in the nighttime, so I decided to spend the rest of the night in the rest room.

F. _____ My heart was racing, and I prayed that the door was strong.

G. _____ I never want to go camping again.

H. _____ It was about 3:00 A.M., and I had to go to the rest room, which was on the top of the hill, approximately thirty yards away from our tents.

I. _____ This warning frightened me, but several days passed, and all was fine.

J. _____ The bear came closer to the rest room and started sniffing around it.

Adapted from a composition by Tiopa Techiryan

1. Which sentence was the most successful in drawing you into the action? _____

2. Have you had any similar experiences? Explain.

_____

_____

_____

YOUR TURN TO WRITE

Step 1: Preparing to Write

WARMING UP: RESPONDING TO OTHERS' WRITING

An excellent way to warm up to writing your own composition is for you to write a response to one of the sample compositions. Look at this example based on the student writing on page 31.

Terror Times Two

Gema Martinez wrote that the most terrifying day of her life happened   1
when her young daughter had an accident in the kitchen. On that day, hot
cooking oil spilled on the child's legs, burning her severely. When Gema
rushed her daughter to the hospital, an administrator at the hospital accused
her of child abuse. Of course, this added to Gema's anguish. Gema had
two reasons to feel terrible. First, she felt awful that the accident happened
in the first place, and second, she felt horrified that someone would accuse
her of child abuse. I can really sympathize with Gema's anguish.

Even though Gema was not guilty of child abuse, many children,
unfortunately, are abused, so I'm glad that the hospital made every effort to   2
investigate this case. Even though innocent people such as Gema
sometimes may be unjustly accused, others who really are guilty of child
abuse can be discovered. This is only because the hospital employees look
into cases that are suspicious to them.

In my opinion, child abuse is a serious social problem and must be
investigated in all cases where even a slight suspicion exists. I believe   3
Gema eventually will forgive the hospital administrator for the mistake
in her case.

YOUR TURN

Using the model in the Warming Up section, write a composition based on one of the sample compositions at the beginning of this chapter. Include three parts:

1. A statement to identify the sample composition
2. A summary of the most important ideas
3. A response: your ideas or opinions, based on the ideas in the composition

SELECTING A TOPIC

With your instructor's guidance, identify a personal experience that

1. occurred in a short period of time in the past.
2. you have a strong emotion or opinion about.
3. you can describe in moment-to-moment, detailed action.

EXPLORING IDEAS

Brainstorming. Brainstorming consists of asking yourself questions about your topic. You can use the basic question words to help you get started.

Who . . . ?	What . . . ?
When . . . ?	How . . . ?
Where . . . ?	Why . . . ?

For example, if your assignment is to write about an embarrassing situation, you might ask yourself the following questions:

Who was involved in the situation?
When did it take place?
Where did it take place?
What happened?
How did you feel about it?
Why did you feel the way you did about it?

Answer these questions in brief note form on paper.

Who was involved?	my family and I
When?	2 yrs. ago
Where?	Korean barbecue restaurant
What happened?	ate dinner, Mom got change for tip, we paid and left, in the parking lot the waiter asked us about the food, no tip, Mom forgot tip, I gave the tip
How did I feel?	very embarrassed
Why did I feel this way?	I felt like a fugitive.

Discussing Your Experience with Others. With a partner or in a small group, tell what your experience is, how you felt about it, and why you chose it. If time allows, explain your experience in moment-to-moment, detailed action. After you finish telling about your experience, ask your partner or group if your strongest emotion or opinion is clear. As an alternative, you can do this outside of class with family or friends.

Step 2: Planning and Organizing

MAKING A ROUGH OUTLINE

Make a rough outline, with key ideas in time order. Leave out any ideas that do not contribute to your main idea. Use the following outline format as a guide.

OUTLINE

Main idea

    Event   _____

                   _____

    Comment   _____

                   _____

Body

    Background
    information   _____

                   _____

    Action/Details   _____

                   _____

                   _____

                   _____

                   _____

                   _____

Conclusion   _____

                   _____

                   _____

                   _____

Step 3: *Writing the First Draft*

Using your notes and outline, write your first draft. As you did in Chapter 1, focus on content and organization, and worry about grammar later — in the second or final draft. Make sure that all of your material explains and supports your main idea. See Appendix, page 227.

Step 4: *Revising*

A common mistake when writing a composition is including irrelevant material. Sentences that do not support the main idea are irrelevant. These have to be rewritten or deleted from the paragraph.

In the composition below, the underlined sentences are irrelevant. They should be eliminated.

A Disappointment in My Brother

Last summer I was very disappointed with my younger brother because of his bad judgment. My brother had come from Austria to visit us on his vacation. He was staying for three weeks during his school vacation, and then he was planning to return to Austria for the next school term. I had not seen him for two years, so I was happy he was visiting. One day he was in the backyard playing with our younger nephew. They went into the storage shed. I could see them from my bedroom. I was reading a novel at the time. I glanced up occasionally to look outside, but I was not spying on them. I was just curious. When they did not come out for a long time, I got curious and decided to see what they were doing. What I saw was a horror! In the middle of the shed was a fire. They were burning small cars and gum. When I saw the fire, I was furious! I was so disappointed in my brother because he was eighteen years old and should have known better than to show fire to a small kid. From then on, it was hard to trust my brother again.

Adapted from a composition by Teresa Poteranska

Discussion

The underlined sentences beginning "He was staying . . ." are not necessary for us to understand the action that follows. The underlined sentences beginning "I was reading . . ." contain details that do not add to the action or support the comment.

 **PRACTICE**

Cross out the five irrelevant sentences in the following composition. Then, with your classmates, discuss why these sentences are not necessary.

Terror in a Car

Five years ago in high school, I had a terrifying experience when two men kidnapped me. ~~I went to a small Catholic high school.~~ I was a B student, and I had a lot of friends. I was on my way home from school when a man in a car approached me and asked, "Excuse me, do you know where Cuahutemoc Street is?" This street was not very far from where we were. It has a lot of stores on it where I like to shop. I gave him directions, but before I finished, another man pulled me into the car, and we took off in a hurry. I started to argue with the men, but one of them shouted, "Shut up, or I'll kill you!" He put a jackknife against my stomach. I stopped protesting.

1

For the next six hours, we drove around the city. During that time, I was scared I might die, and I thought about my entire life: my parents, my friends, everything. The men were discussing what they were going to do with me. Finally one said, "Let her go. I think this is enough." Later they left me on an abandoned and isolated road. I did not know what to do. It was nighttime, and I was really scared.

2

Luckily, a taxi came by and took me home. The taxi was an old Ford with lumpy seats. When my parents saw me, they hugged and kissed me. It felt so wonderful to be safe again. I hope nobody else will have to experience the kind of terror I felt that day.

3

Adapted from a composition by Keyla Moreno

Read Keyla's composition again, this time without the irrelevant sentences. Why is it better than it was before?

_____

_____

_____

YOUR TURN

Review your draft to revise it. Look for irrelevant material and eliminate it from your paragraph. You may do the revision by peer response or/and self-evaluation.

PEER RESPONSE

You may remember from Chapter 1 that peer response gives you valuable practice and useful input.

When you exchange drafts with your partner, follow these general guidelines:

1. Read your partner's draft twice. The second time you read it, discuss any unclear spots with him or her.
2. Check the draft for clear organization. Refer to the Checkpoints for Revision that follows. Point out any possible problems to your partner.
3. What information or details would you like to know that your partner has not included? Tell your partner what you would like to know. Then your partner can consider adding this information.

SELF-EVALUATION

Analyze your own draft to improve the content and organization. As you may recall from Chapter 1, the best way to do this is to set your draft aside for at least twenty-four hours so that you can evaluate it with a fresh mind. Refer to Checkpoints for Revision, which follows.

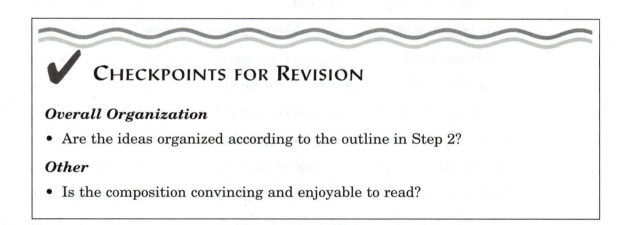

✔ CHECKPOINTS FOR REVISION

Overall Organization
- Are the ideas organized according to the outline in Step 2?

Other
- Is the composition convincing and enjoyable to read?

Step 5: Proofreading and Editing

PRACTICE

Edit the following draft. Find these errors.

	Number of Errors to Find
Spelling	2
Missing subject	1
Missing verb	2
Run-on sentence	1
Sentence fragment	1
Present or past tense	4

Dinner with Thirty Grandparents

About two months ago, my friend Song and I spent an embarrassing
evening at a popular local restaurant. Song came from San Francisco
to visit me in Los Angeles for the weekend, and we ~~decide~~ *decided* to go out to
diner at a nice restaurant.

We went to Alpine Village in Torrance because I had heard that the food
was especially delicious there. When we enter the restaurant, we pleased
right away because the atmosphere was good, and the waitresses were very
kind. We took a seat and ordered our meals.

About five minutes later, I looked around more carefully and realized
that Song and I were the only teenagers their. Almost everybody else was
at least over fifty years old. Feeling uncomfortable, we started eating. As
fast as we could. While we were eating, one of the waitresses approach
us and said, "There several young ladies nearby looking for dance
partners." I turned to look at the "young ladies," they looked old enough to
be our mothers or grandmothers. This make us eat even faster.

While we were paying the bill, the cashier commented to us, "So, do
you guys enjoy having dinner with thirty grandparents?" We smiled with
embarrassment and left as quickly as could.

Adapted from a composition by Nick Yang

In your opinion, what makes Nick's composition successful?

_____

_____

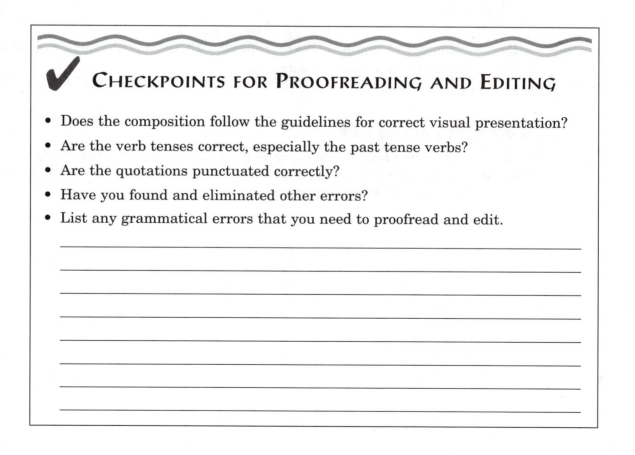

YOUR TURN

Proofread and edit your draft for grammar and visual presentation. You may do this by peer response and/or self-evaluation.

PEER RESPONSE

As noted in Chapter 1 peer response gives you valuable practice and useful input.
Exchange drafts with your partner. Read your partner's draft twice. The second time you read it, point out possible errors to him or her. Refer to Checkpoints for Proofreading and Editing, which follows.

SELF-EVALUATION

Proofread and edit your own draft. As you probably remember, you should set your draft aside for at least twenty-four hours before you do this step. Refer to Checkpoints for Proofreading and Editing, which follows.

✔ CHECKPOINTS FOR PROOFREADING AND EDITING

- Does the composition follow the guidelines for correct visual presentation?
- Are the verb tenses correct, especially the past tense verbs?
- Are the quotations punctuated correctly?
- Have you found and eliminated other errors?
- List any grammatical errors that you need to proofread and edit.

_____

_____

_____

_____

_____

_____

_____

_____

_____

Step 6: *Writing the Final Draft*

Write your final draft with the revisions and corrections. After you finish, proofread and edit it again carefully.

Step 7: *Following Up and Evaluating Progress*

SHARING YOUR WRITING WITH OTHERS

Traveling Compositions. You will do this activity before you turn in your final draft to the instructor. Follow these steps:

1. Exchange your composition with a classmate. Repeat this step with other classmates several times. In this way, your composition will "travel" across the classroom.
2. Read the composition that "traveled" into your hands.
3. At the end of the composition, write a positive comment — a sentence or two — about the content.

   Possible comments:

   > I enjoyed reading your ideas.
   > I have a similar point of view.
   > I've had an experience like yours.
   > You've really convinced me about . . .
   > I admire your . . .
   > I like . . .

   Do not comment on organization or grammar. Do not say anything negative.
4. Sign your name after your comment.
5. Return the composition.

BENEFITING FROM FEEDBACK

After your instructor returns your composition to you, continue looking for patterns of your strengths and weaknesses. This way you can focus on building on your strengths and on how to overcome your weaknesses.

Ideas for Writing

Write about one of the following situations.

1. *An embarrassing situation in a new culture.* This could be a cultural misunderstanding or a language problem.

2. *An embarrassing experience of any kind*

3. *A funny situation.* Often, a funny situation comes about from an embarrassing situation or a misunderstanding, but it can also develop from any situation that you can look back on and laugh about now.

4. *A frightening or terrifying situation.* Think back to childhood for an example of a frightening situation. Even though the childhood situation may not seem frightening to you any longer, try to put yourself back in time to remember the fear you felt then, and recreate this feeling in your composition. You could also write about a frightening situation you experienced as an adult. For example: a dangerous experience on a vacation, being the victim of a crime, and so forth. (Do not describe a nightmare; the experience must be a real-life experience.)

5. *A situation in which you felt proud of yourself.* The word "pride" can have both positive and negative meanings. For this assignment, think of "pride" in the positive sense. Did you accomplish a personal goal? Did you win a contest? Did you perform in a play or music recital? Did your team win an important game? Did your child accomplish something special?

6. *Your first impression in a new culture.* For this topic, you need to decide on a comment and then select an experience or event that is limited in time. The body of your composition will then explain your feeling or opinion in specific detail.

7. *A frustrating situation.* For example: a bad day at home, at school, in traffic, shopping, and so forth.

8. *A situation in which you experienced total joy, peace, or other pleasant emotion*

9. *A situation in which you experienced panic over a minor problem that was easily resolved*

10. *A situation in which you experienced disappointment*

11. *A situation in which you struggled with a challenge or problem and found the courage to solve it*

12. *A first-day experience.* This could be a first day at school, a place of worship, or a new job; the first time riding a bicycle, driving a car, or playing soccer (or another sport); the first time using a computer, or traveling in an airplane, or on a boat. Make sure you can provide a comment.

13. *A sad day in your life.* This could be the day you lost someone or something you loved, a funeral, or other unhappy event.

14. *An incident that taught you a valuable lesson*

15. *A traumatic experience*

16. *A natural disaster or an accident*

17. *A shocking experience*

18. *The experience in the comic strip below*

19. *Your own idea.* If you have an idea for a topic, present it to your instructor. He or she will determine if it is appropriate for this assignment.

Important: You need your instructor's approval before you start your assignment.

"Calvin and Hobbes" by Bill Watterson. © 1995 Watterson. Dist. by Universal Press Syndicate. Reprinted with permission. All rights reserved.

CHAPTER *3*

Providing Examples

In this chapter, you will use examples to explain and support your main idea. An *example* provides a specific illustration of your main idea and develops it with specific, supporting details.

Do you know anyone who is extremely forgetful?

Sample 1

How Can He Forget That?

My Uncle Quang often forgets things. For example, two months ago, my grandfather asked him to go to the post office to send a package to one of our relatives. Uncle Quang said he would mail it, but when he returned from the post office, he announced that he forgot to take the package with him. My grandfather was very disappointed. 1

Another time, when Uncle Quang took me to a Vietnamese restaurant, his forgetfulness made me feel very embarrassed. While he was dressing, I asked him if he had his money in his pants pocket, because he usually forgets his wallet when he changes pants. When it was time to pay our bill, Uncle Quang discovered that his wallet wasn't in his pocket after all. The waiter stared at us while Uncle Quang desperately searched all his pockets. I wanted to disappear. 2

Another example of Uncle Quang's forgetfulness took place recently when my grandmother asked him to take the family to the airport. Everyone was ready to go, but he couldn't remember where his car keys were. In a rush, we looked everywhere in the house for the keys. Then my aunt asked him, "Have you checked your pocket?" That's exactly where the keys were! The sight of my uncle finding his keys in his pocket made us laugh, and our anger disappeared. If anyone knows of a treatment for forgetfulness, please let me know. Uncle Quang really could use some help. 3

Adapted from a composition by Vu Dang

1. For you, which of Vu's three examples is the most convincing? Why?

   _____

   _____

   _____

2. Have you had any similar experiences? Explain.

   _____

   _____

   _____

Do phone calls ever cause you an inconvenience?

Sample 2

Wrong Number

Phone calls for the wrong number seem to come at very inconvenient 1
times. For example, a week ago I just got comfortable with a snack and a
movie when suddenly the phone rang. As I was running to answer it, I
tripped over the dog and fell hitting my nose on the carpet. When I got to
the phone and picked it up, a strange voice asked for Julie.

I also get wrong numbers when I'm taking a bath. For instance, yesterday 2
I was enjoying a nice bubble bath when, of course, the phone rang. At first, I
didn't move, but then I thought that it might be an important call. I grabbed a
towel and rushed to the phone, just in time to hear a voice ask, "Is this
Radio Shack?"

Probably the most annoying time to get a wrong number is when I'm 3
cooking. One time the person calling couldn't believe that he got the
wrong number, and he kept arguing with me about names. I hung up
furiously and rushed back to my overcooked eggs. Well, I've had enough,
so I'm asking for a telephone answering machine for my next birthday.

Adapted from a composition by Valerie Redon Gabel

1. For you, which of Valerie's three examples is the most convincing?
   Why? _____
   _____

2. Have you had any similar experiences? Explain.
   _____
   _____

Are there any activities in your everyday life that you dislike because they
waste a lot of your time?

Sample 3

Wasting Time

I hate wasting my time. For instance, shopping is often a waste of time, 1
especially when I'm looking for a gift. It takes a lot of time to find something
I like and can afford. The last time I went shopping for a gift, I spent at least
three hours looking in stores before I found something appropriate.

Another example of a time waster is cooking. I have to cook for my family, but I'm not a good cook. Furthermore, everyone in my family likes a different kind of food. One likes chicken, another likes seafood, and still another likes pasta. I cook whatever everyone likes because I want them all to enjoy their meal. It takes about two hours every evening to prepare dinner. Sometimes I wish I could just order take-out food.

2

As a last example, relying on the bus for transportation wastes my time. I take the bus to school every day. It takes me ten minutes to walk to the bus stop, twenty minutes to ride on the bus, and another fifteen minutes to walk from the bus stop to school. That's a total of forty-five minutes! If I had a car, it would take me only ten to fifteen minutes. I wish I had a servant to shop for me, cook for me, and take me to school.

3

Adapted from a composition by Lan Ho

1. For you, which of Lan's three examples is the most convincing? Why?

_____

_____

2. Do you have any similar opinions? Explain.

_____

_____

What are some common examples of culture shock that people in an unfamiliar culture may experience?

Sample 4

Culture Shock in Germany

Even though German culture is similar to my own background in many ways, I still suffered from culture shock during my vacation in Germany a few years ago. For example, people drive very fast on German freeways because there is no speed limit. I was driving at least seventy miles per hour, but most of the traffic passed me as though I were standing still. What really made me uncomfortable, though, was that the traffic behind me honked impatiently.

1

For another example, whenever I bought something at a store, I would hold my palm open for the change, but the clerk would ignore my hand and put the change on the counter. After this happened several times, I wondered if the clerks were being rude to me because I was an American. Later I realized that the problem was a difference in customs.

2

The most upsetting example of culture shock happened when I went   3
shopping for fruit in a grocery store. I was selecting my fruit and putting it into
a paper bag, when a large German woman ran toward me screaming. I
honestly didn't know what the problem was. It turned out that customers are
not allowed to select their own fruit. Instead, the clerk is supposed to choose
it and put it into a bag for you. Even though these examples seem like
trivial incidents, all together they made me uneasy until I realized that I was
experiencing a normal case of culture shock.

1. For you, which of the three examples is the most convincing? Why?

   _____

   _____

2. Have you had any similar experiences? Explain.

   _____

   _____

Are there any gestures that have caused you embarrassment in an unfamiliar
culture? Give examples.

Sample 5

Embarrassing Gestures

Three common North American gestures often cause embarrassment   1
to foreign students. First, North Americans commonly express "OK" by
touching the tip of the index finger with the tip of the thumb, forming a
circle. This gesture indicates approval, but in some cultures, it means a rude
word.

Another embarrassing gesture is what North Americans call "the bird."   2
For many foreign students, it's natural to point with the middle finger, but for
North Americans, this gesture is very insulting. Foreign students are stared
at and laughed at when they point with the middle finger, and it's very
embarrassing for them when they find out why.

Still another very embarrassing gesture is the North American "good   3
luck" sign, with index and middle fingers crossed. For English speakers, this
is a sign of giving encouragement to someone, but for people from some
parts of the word, it refers to the sex act. Gestures vary from culture to
culture, and foreign students need to be aware of these differences in order
to avoid embarrassment.

1. Have you had any uncomfortable experiences because of any of the above gestures? Which one(s)? Explain.

_____

_____

2. Are there any other gestures you could add to the examples given above? Explain.

_____

_____

LOOKING AT CONTENT AND ORGANIZATION

The Main Idea

A clear main idea includes a topic and a comment. The topic is who or what the composition is about. The comment is the writer's opinion, emotion, or other idea about the topic.

Topic:	A characteristic of my Uncle Quang
Comment:	He often forgets things.

My Uncle Quang often forgets things.

Topic:	Phone calls for the wrong number
Comment:	They seem to come at very inconvenient times.

Phone calls for the wrong number seem to come at very inconvenient times.

 **PRACTICE**

Write main ideas for the following topics. (Suggestions appear in parentheses.)

1. A friend or relative (Identify the person and give a dominant characteristic.)
   My cousin Smilla is very kind to animals. _____

2. Neighbor(s) (Identify him/her/them and give a dominant characteristic.)

   _____

   _____

3. Culture shock (Identify the person who has experienced culture shock and the situation.)

_____

_____

4. Luck (Identify the person and the type of luck — either good *or* bad. Also, give a general time period, such as "last week," "lately," "in the last six months.")

_____

_____

5. Pet peeves[†] (Identify the person and include a qualifier such as "several" or "three.")

_____

_____

[†]Pet peeves = annoyances in everyday life

The Body

The body of your composition is organized into detailed examples. One common way to organize the order of the examples is to put the most important or most convincing example last. Another way to organize is to put the examples in time order. In Sample 1 "How Can He Forget That?" Vu supported his main idea with the following examples:

1. For example, two months ago, my grandfather asked him to go to the post office to send a package …

2. Another time, when Uncle Quang took me to a Vietnamese restaurant, his forgetfulness …

3. Another example of Uncle Quang's forgetfulness took place recently when my grandmother …

The time signals "two months ago" and "recently" suggest that Vu used time order.

PRACTICE A

Read Samples 2 through 5 again. Then, with your classmates, decide how each writer organized the examples.

A. Most important/convincing last   OR

B. Time order

Sample 2: _____

Sample 3: _____

Sample 4: _____

Sample 5: _____

PRACTICE B

First, list three examples of the forgetfulness of someone you know. As an alternative, you may use your imagination and create the person and examples. Then, number the examples in the order you would put them in a composition.

Examples of Forgetfulness   *Order of Examples*

_____   _____

_____   _____

_____   _____

On what basis did you select the above order? Circle one.

Most important/convincing last   OR   Time

The Conclusion

The conclusion of your composition ties together the entire piece as in the following three examples:

1. If anyone knows of a treatment for forgetfulness, please let me know. Uncle Quang could use some help.

2. Well, I've had enough, so I'm asking for a telephone answering machine for my next birthday.

3. I wish I had a servant to shop for me, cook for me, and take me to school.

Write a conclusion for each of the following paragraphs.

Composition A

My Supportive Family

My family supports my decision to go back to school in the evenings. Everyone helps and contributes in some way. For example, my husband takes me to school and picks me up because the parking is terrible. Besides, he doesn't want me to walk alone in the parking lot at night. Also, my children help by taking turns doing the dinner dishes, since I don't have time in the evenings anymore. Even my sister helps out. Since she finished her B.A. degree last year, she has encouraged me and given me advice when I have papers to write.

_____

_____

_____

Composition B

My Noisy Neighbors

My happy, peaceful world ended six months ago when my new neighbors moved in. They make a lot of noise. For example, they have loud parties three or four times a week. During these parties they play loud heavy metal music, so the guests have to shout to each other. All this noise continues until the early hours of the morning, and I can fall asleep only after the party is over. They also have three dogs that bark almost all the time. This really bothers me in the evening after I have been working and going to school all day. I want to rest, but I can't. All of this is bad enough, but worst of all for me is that the husband and wife fight a lot. Most of the time they don't see eye to eye, and they end up arguing. Then, their kids get scared and start crying. It's impossible for me to study or even to think rationally during all this.

_____

_____

_____

Adapted from a composition by Ni Ni Mar

LANGUAGE TIPS

Signals

Signals are words or expressions that help the reader follow your ideas from one example to the next. In the following examples, the signals are underlined.

> For example, two months ago, my grandfather asked him (Uncle Quang) to go to the post office ...

> Another time, when Uncle Quang said he would take me to a Vietnamese restaurant ...

> Another example of Uncle Quang's forgetfulness took place recently when ...

 PRACTICE

List additional signals from Samples 2 through 5 at the beginning of this chapter.

_____

_____

_____

_____

_____

_____

_____

_____

_____

_____

PRACTICING WHAT YOU HAVE LEARNED

Use your imagination and write the missing details in the following compositions in the spaces provided.

Composition A

A Dangerous Driver

My friend Otto drives dangerously. For example, last week _a police_
officer stopped Otto on the freeway for _____

_____

_____

_____

_____

_____

Another time when Otto was giving me a ride to work, _____

_____

_____

_____

_____

_____

_____

_____

The most frightening example of Otto's dangerous driving happened a few days ago. _____

_____

_____

_____

_____

The next time I go somewhere with Otto, I'll offer to drive.

In the following composition, fill in the details, including an appropriate title. At the end write a conclusion.

Composition B

_____

My third cousin Fanny is the messiest person I know. I discovered this when she came to visit our family for a week last month. For example, one day after she had made a sandwich for herself in the kitchen, I walked in and found

_____

_____

_____

_____

As another example of her messiness, on another day when she got back from shopping, she _____

_____

_____

_____

The clearest example of the problem happened in the bathroom. Every day she _____

_____

_____

_____

_____

(conclusion) _____

_____

YOUR TURN TO WRITE

Step 1: Preparing to Write

SELECTING A TOPIC

With your instructor's guidance, choose a topic that you are familiar with and that you can develop with specific detailed examples.

EXPLORING IDEAS

Freewriting. On a sheet of paper, start writing freely about your topic. Allow your mind to explore, and write everything that comes to mind, without judging or censoring anything.

You will find that one idea leads to another. In this way, you will discover useful ideas that you may have otherwise overlooked. Do not worry about correct grammar or spelling.

If you get stuck, simply write "I'm thinking about (my topic), and the ideas are starting to come to me" over and over until the ideas start to come to you.

Example of Freewriting

> Noise pollution in the city
>
> I'm thinking about noise pollution in the city, and the ideas are starting to come to me. Noise. Car alarms. Leaf blowers. Cars with loud music. Screaming music. Why do people like to attract attention like that? What about their hearing? My uncle says they'll go deaf. Don't they know it bothers other people? Loud systems cost a lot, too. Some cities have laws against loud boom boom music. Also, some cities have laws against leaf blowers. But gardeners are just doing their job. Barking dogs. My neighbor has a big dog that stays alone all day in a small yard. Poor dog! I feel sorry for it. Isn't there a law against barking dogs, too? If not, there should be. Building construction. They're building an apartment in the lot near my house. Saws, pounding nails, cement trucks, shouting. Some people are inconsiderate, but others are just doing their job.

Discussing Your Topic with Others. With a partner or in a small group, take turns telling about your topic. If time allows, give detailed examples to support your main idea. After you finish, ask your partner or group if your main idea is clear and if your examples clearly support your main idea. As an alternative, you can do this outside of class with family or friends. See Appendix 2, page 225.

Step 2: Planning and Organizing

MAKING A ROUGH OUTLINE

Make a rough outline, with key ideas in effective order. Use this outline format as a guide.

OUTLINE

Main idea _____

_____

Example 1 _____

_____

_____

_____

Example 2 _____

_____

_____

_____

Example 3 _____

_____

_____

_____

Conclusion _____

_____

Step 3: *Writing the First Draft*

Write your first draft, using the ideas you gathered as a result of your freewriting and your outline. As before, focus on content and organization. Make sure that your examples consist of specific, supporting details. See Appendix 2, page 227.

Step 4: *Revising*

PRACTICE

Revise the following composition. Add a main idea, one signal, details for one point, and write a conclusion.

My Recent Bad Luck

_____ 1

To start out, last Sunday I was at the mall shopping for new shoes. I decided on a pair, and the clerk put the information into the cash register. When I wanted to write a check, I discovered that my last check was gone, and I didn't have enough cash, either. I was very embarrassed. I couldn't find my car in the parking lot. My last example of bad luck is my worst. Last Thursday morning, I got into a car accident. Although I woke up very late that morning, I still thought I could make my eight o'clock class on time if I hurried. So, what of all things happened on that day? My 1987 Toyota wouldn't start. I don't know how many times I repeated, "Please, come on!" Once I got the car started, I had to rush to be on time because I only had ten minutes to spare. I stepped on the accelerator very hard. Suddenly, there was a big noise, and my car stopped completely. I didn't see the driver in the car in front of me put on his brakes.

_____
_____

YOUR TURN

Review your draft for ways to revise it. You may do this by peer response and/or self-evaluation.

Exchange compositions with your partner. Follow these general guidelines:

1. Read your partner's draft twice. The second time you read it, discuss any unclear spots with your partner.
2. Check the paper for clear organization. Refer to the Checkpoints for Revision that follows. Point out any possible problems.
3. What information or details would you like to know that your partner has not included in the paper? Tell your partner what you would like to know. Then your partner can consider adding this information to the paper.

SELF-EVALUATION

Analyze your own draft for ways to improve the content and organization. Refer to Checkpoints for Revision, which follows.

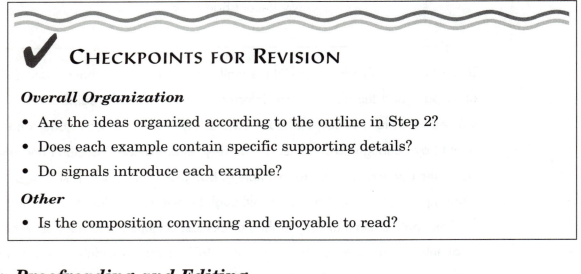

✔ CHECKPOINTS FOR REVISION

Overall Organization

- Are the ideas organized according to the outline in Step 2?
- Does each example contain specific supporting details?
- Do signals introduce each example?

Other

- Is the composition convincing and enjoyable to read?

Step 5: Proofreading and Editing

PRACTICE

Edit the draft on the opposite page. Find these errors.

	Number of Errors to Find
Spelling	1
Missing subject	2
Missing verb	2
Run-on sentence	1
Sentence fragment	2
Present or past tense	3

A Pet Peeve: Misleading Packaging

^{am}
I tired of purchasing everything from cookies to cosmetics. Only to find 1
when I get home that I've been cheated. The problem trick packaging. For
example, when I buy a bottle of juice or other liquid. Often I discover that 3
the contents look greater than they really are because the glass is so thick,
or the bottom of the bottle not flat. 5

As another example of trick packaging, recently I bought a package of
Nibble Star cookies that look twice as full as the package next to it on the 7
shelf at Lucky Shopper. When I got home and opened the package, I
discover that the tray holding the cookies take up more room in the box than 9
the cookies. What I was paying for was a lot of plastic that just took up more
room in my trash. 11

The clearest example of trick packaging is the way toys appear in there
boxes, they look so much bigger and better than really are. Recently my 13
nephew wanted a Power Ranger doll that looked tall and strong in its
colorful box. When we got it home and looked at it more closely, we found 15
that it was tiny and made of flimsy plastic. Buyers really have to be careful
to make sure don't get fooled by trick packaging. 17

YOUR TURN

Proofread and edit your draft for grammar and visual presentation. You may do this by peer response and/or self-evaluation.

PEER RESPONSE AND/OR SELF-EVALUATION

Exchange drafts with your partner. Read your partner's draft twice. The second time you read it, point out possible errors. Refer to Checkpoints for Proofreading and Editing, which follows.

Proofread and edit your own draft. Refer to Checkpoints for Proofreading and Editing on page 64.

Step 6: Writing the Final Draft

Write your final draft with the revisions and corrections. After you finish, proofread and edit it again carefully.

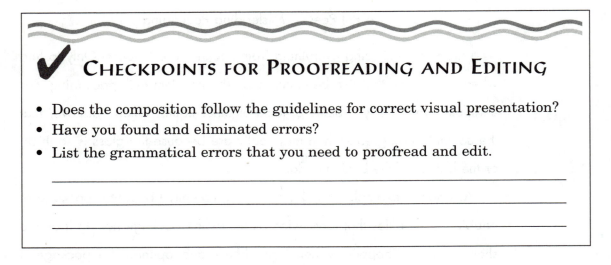

- Does the composition follow the guidelines for correct visual presentation?
- Have you found and eliminated errors?
- List the grammatical errors that you need to proofread and edit.

_____

_____

_____

Step 7: *Following Up and Evaluating Your Progress*

WINDING DOWN: RESPONDING TO YOUR CLASSMATES' WRITING

Before you turn in your final draft, exchange compositions with a classmate, and write a composition based on your partner's composition. Include the following:

1. A statement to identify your partner's composition
2. A summary of the most important ideas
3. A response: your ideas or opinions, based on the ideas in the composition.

Example of a Summary and Response

Forgetfulness: A Medical Problem?

In "How Can He Forget That?" Vu Dang gives three examples of his Uncle Quang's forgetfulness. In all three examples, Uncle Quang's forgetfulness is harmless. Perhaps he has inconvenienced and embarrassed his family, but no one has gotten hurt. In fact, the situations Vu describes are almost humorous. When I read Vu's words, I could imagine the family's affection for Uncle Quang and their forgiveness of his minor faults. 1

Reading about Uncle Quang reminded me of my Aunt May. Ten years ago she began forgetting things, similar to the kinds of things Vu's Uncle Quang forgot. About five years ago, Aunt May's forgetfulness got worse, and often she would go for a walk in the neighborhood, get lost, and wander out into the streets. Out of concern, my cousin took his mother to the doctor, and the doctor told him that Aunt May probably has Alzheimer's disease. 2

Maybe Uncle Quang is forgetful by nature. On the other hand, maybe Uncle Quang has a medical problem. In any case, it might be worth a visit to a doctor for a medical evaluation. 3

BENEFITING FROM FEEDBACK

After your instructor returns your composition, continue looking for your patterns of strengths and weaknesses. At this point, you probably know what some of these are.

Now is the time to start working on eliminating your weaknesses. This means a commitment on your part to review and study independently. If you need help, talk with your instructor. See Appendix 2, page 231.

Ideas for Writing

① Quiz
② JOURNAL
③ HW
④ group work - book
⑤ time order/importance

Write about one of the following topics.

Personal Topics

1. *Examples of certain characteristics of a person you know.* Possible characteristics: generosity, honesty, clumsiness, forgetfulness, perfectionism, consideration, pessimism, optimism, inconsideration, messiness, kindness, helpfulness, rudeness, laziness, stubbornness, irresponsibility, shyness, friendliness, and so forth.

   Example of a main idea:

   > My neighbor Hannibal is inconsiderate of the other people in our neighborhood.

2. *Examples of your recent good (or bad) luck*
3. *Examples of difficult or time-consuming homework assignments* you've had lately
4. *Examples of grammar points (or other features of English) that you find confusing*
5. *Examples of ways you have helped someone, or ways someone has helped you*

Nonpersonal Topics

6. *Examples of noise pollution in the city*

7. *Typical examples of culture shock for foreign students* from one particular country or area of the world

8. *Examples of violence on television (or in the movies)*

9. *Examples of exciting visual effects in movies*

10. *Examples of increasing crime in this city / town / area, or examples of effective crime control*

11. *Examples of ridiculous (or attractive) fashions currently in style*

12. *Examples of advertising tricks*

13. *Examples of rudeness (or politeness) in drivers in the city / town / area where you live*

14. *Examples of political corruption or political effectiveness*

15. *Examples of television programs that are good (or bad) for children*

16. *Examples of unnecessary (or necessary) wars*

17. *Examples of prejudice* (You will need to limit this topic.)

Your Own Idea

18. If you have an idea for a topic, present it to your instructor. He or she will determine if it is appropriate for this assignment.

Important: You need your instructor's approval before you start your assignment.

CHAPTER **4**

Supplying Reasons

In this chapter, you will select a main idea that raises the question "Why?" The support, then, will consist of reasons and specific, supporting details that answer the question "Why?"

Note: A reason is also called a *point*. (Other types of points are covered in the next chapter.)

Do you have a hobby that you enjoy a lot? Why do you enjoy it?

Sample 1

My Wonderful Harmonica

    I love to play my harmonica whenever I can. One reason that I enjoy   1
it so much is that it relaxes me. Because it is so small, I can take my lovely,
little harmonica wherever I go, such as to school. I can put it in my book bag,
and then, if I have a break between classes, I can play it in the car for a few
minutes and feel peaceful in the middle of my busy day.

    Next, the harmonica is so easy to play. It is as simple as singing a song.   2
When I hear a new song that I like, I can pick up my harmonica and play
the tune right away. Also, the sound is so romantic. Imagine that you hear

the sound of a harmonica in the middle of the night coming from somewhere. It might remind you of a lover calling to his special lady.

The most important reason I treasure my harmonica is that when I   3
see or touch it, I can feel my father's love. He gave me a shiny, new harmonica as a birthday present ten years ago, and he often wanted me to play it for him. So, playing my harmonica reminds me of my father. I thank my father for introducing me to this wonderful hobby, and I will probably give one to my own son some day.

Adapted from a composition by Jee Moon

In your opinion, which of Jee's reasons is the most convincing? Why?

_____

_____

_____

Have you made any important decisions in the past few years? What was the decision, and what are your reasons behind your decision?

Sample 2

Freedom

The decision to immigrate to the United States from Somalia was not a   1
difficult one for me. First of all, I knew I could continue my education here. It is very expensive to go to college in Somalia, so when I graduated from high school, I decided to find a place where I could afford to continue studying.

Another reason I immigrated to this country was to have the freedom to   2
choose my own marriage partner. In Somalia, a young woman's parents might fix her up with somebody she has never seen, and then they want her to get married in a matter of days. I don't think there can be any love in this kind of marriage. If the young woman does not marry the person chosen for her, her parents often get angry and exclude her from the family. When I get married, I want to marry for love.

The most important reason I moved to this country is for freedom   3
of speech. This became very important to me five years ago when my family suffered a terrible tragedy. My uncle was in a bar, having fun with his friends. While they were discussing politics, he said that the president of the country was a "big mouth." Because of this statement, some police officers beat my uncle to death. I will never forget this injustice for the rest

of my life. In short, the reason I left my country to find a new home was to live in freedom.

Adapted from a composition by Maryam Alasow

In your opinion, which of Maryam's reasons is the most convincing? Why?

_____

_____

_____

Have you made any important buying decisions recently? What did you decide to buy, and what are your reasons for buying that item?

Sample 3

Why I Bought a Computer

Three months ago I decided to buy a computer for several wonderful reasons. First, I think it is much easier to type on a keyboard than it is to write by hand. I got tired of my slow handwriting and the messiness of erasers and liquid paper.

Another reason is that I wanted to get a grammar checker and a spell checker. If I have errors in grammar and spelling, the computer can show me how to correct these problems. Next, the printouts from a computer are easier to read than my handwriting, and I can use various styles of print, such as italics and bold letters. I can even use different sizes or shapes of letters according to my mood. If I want to, I can even use decorations.

The most important reason I decided to get a computer is that I can save all my projects as "files." This means that I can see my files again whenever I want. I cannot memorize all my ideas, but I can store them in the computer. The computer becomes like a part of my brain. Since I can save my files, I can revise and edit my assignments more easily. For me, a computer is the best purchase I have ever made.

Adapted from a composition by Young Bae

In your opinion, which of Young's reasons is the most convincing? Why?

_____

_____

_____

Have you taken any trips in recent years? How did you feel about the trip, and why did you feel the way you did?

Sample 4

Paris: My Dream Come True

Ten years ago, after years of dreaming about Paris, I finally got to take the trip of my dreams. First of all, we stayed in a great hotel. It overlooked the Seine, the famous river I read about in so many poems. In the morning, my husband and I had café au lait and sweet-smelling, oven-fresh croissants for breakfast while we watched the river go by below. It flowed by very slowly and gave me the feeling that it was telling me the long story of Paris.   1

Next, the Montparnasse, a district in Paris on the left bank of the Seine, was wonderful. Many painters gather here. When we went up the hill, we saw painters from all over the world working on their canvases. The air was filled with the sounds of happy people and the smell of paint.   2

What I enjoyed most, though, were the cafés. One of my favorite dreams was just to sip a cup of coffee at a café in Paris. I had seen so many pictures of those cafés in books, and finally, my dream came true. I really enjoyed watching people walking on the street and listening to them speak French. Some of them had on gorgeous dresses, while others were dressed more casually; but everyone had a sense of chic. I will always remember the wonderful sights, sounds, and smells of Paris.   3

Adapted from a composition by Teruyo Tsuchiya

In your opinion, which of Teruyo's reasons is the most convincing? Why?

_____

_____

_____

What is your opinion about violent programs on television? What are your reasons for this opinion?

Sample 5

Violence on Television

I am not in favor of the large number of violent programs on television these days. First, violence does not provide a good example to children. For instance, cartoons contain violence, and children who watch a lot of cartoons tend to play games that imitate what they see on TV. Later on, they become confused about what is appropriate and what is not.   1

Next, TV violence teaches teenagers models of behavior for their own 2
lives. I have heard several stories on the news about teenagers who got an
idea for a violent act from a show they had seen on TV.

Last, violence on television causes adults to get so used to crime and 3
brutality that they start losing their feelings of horror about it. They begin
accepting it as normal. For all these reasons, I wish producers would reduce
the number of violent shows on television.

Adapted from a composition by Cinthya Volkov

In your opinion, which of Cinthya's reasons is the most convincing? Why?

_____

_____

_____

LOOKING AT CONTENT AND ORGANIZATION

The Main Idea

A clear main idea includes a topic and a comment. For this assignment, the main
idea also raises the question "Why?" in the mind of the reader.

Topic:	My harmonica
Comment:	I love to play it whenever I can.
Why?	Why does he love it so much?

I love to play my harmonica whenever I can.

 PRACTICE A

*In each of the following pairs of sentences, one sentence provides a main idea and
the other provides support. Circle the letter of the main idea in each pair.*

1. A. Soccer gives me a chance to be with my friends.
    B. My favorite hobby is soccer.

2. A. My decision to leave home was one of the hardest decisions I've ever had to make.

    B. My little brother cried when he heard I was thinking about moving out on my own.

3. A. I love living alone in an apartment.

    B. I can keep my place as messy as I want.

4. A. The language barrier presents an enormous challenge.

    B. Living in a foreign country can be difficult.

5. A. Teenagers should wait until they finish school before they get married.

    B. Without an education, it is hard to find a career that pays a decent salary.

6. A. The Metropolitan Museum in New York is a wonderful place to visit.

    B. The museum has a large collection of high-quality paintings.

7. A. It costs a lot to own a dog.

    B. Owning a dog is more trouble than it is worth.

PRACTICE B

Select three of the following topics, and write a main idea for each one. Be as specific as possible.

Topics:	A hobby	A job
	A decision	Pets
	A trip	Smoking

Example

Topic: Pets

Main idea: Owning a dog causes more trouble than it's worth.

1. _____

2. _____

3. _____

The Body

The body of your composition is organized into points and details. Each point gives a reason, and each reason is followed by specific supporting details that explain and develop the reason.

One common way to organize the points is to put the most important or most convincing point last, as in the following example.

The Reasons I Gave up Smoking

After three years of trying to quit smoking, I finally gave up the habit six months ago for several good reasons. To begin with, I got tired of the smell. My hair usually smelled bad, my breath was always sour, and my apartment always smelled like nicotine. Second, I felt uncomfortable when people reacted negatively to my cigarettes. Complete strangers would give me dirty looks and move away from me. Even my girlfriend began to avoid me. Next, cigarettes just kept getting more and more expensive. I estimate that smoking cost me over one hundred dollars a month. The most important reason, though, is that I began to worry about my health. I do not mind having a little cough, but I am really afraid of health problems when I get older, such as cancer and heart disease. No pleasure is worth that price! Now that I have given up smoking, I can enjoy clean air again, people are friendly toward me, I have more spending money, and my cough is gone. Life is just more enjoyable.

1. What are the writer's four reasons for giving up smoking?

   _____

   _____

   _____

   _____

2. In your opinion, which reason is the most convincing? Why?

   _____

   _____

   _____

   _____

 **PRACTICE**

Use your imagination and write details to support the reasons in the composition starting on the next page. You may use examples or any other type of specific details. Read all the sentences given before you begin writing.

Rosco's Fiasco

I'll never eat at Rosco's Rib House again. First of all, the service is terrible.

_____

_____

_____

_____

_____

Another reason I'll never go back is that the atmosphere is unpleasant. _____

_____

_____

_____

_____

_____

_____

What convinced me more than anything else, though, was the food. _____

_____

_____

_____

_____

I don't understand how a place like that can stay in business.

The Conclusion

The conclusion ties together the entire composition. Common kinds of conclusions include a summary of the reasons, a look to the future, or a related thought that grows out of the body, as in the following examples.

Note: Often, a conclusion contains more than one of the above.

A general restatement of the reasons:	In short, the reason I left my country to find a new home was to live in freedom.
A summary of the reasons:	I enjoy clean air again, people are friendly toward me, I have more spending money, and my cough is gone.
A look to the future:	I thank my father for introducing me to this wonderful hobby, and I will probably give one to my own son some day.
A related thought that grows out of the body:	For all these reasons, I wish producers would reduce the number of violent shows on television.

 PRACTICE

Write two to three separate conclusions for the following composition.

A Lousy Place to Live

I hate my apartment. First, the plumbing does not work right. The toilet runs constantly, the sink stops up regularly, and the faucets drip. Next, the neighbors are noisy. They party late into the night, even on week nights, and the landlord does not tell them to quiet down. In fact, he parties along with them. The most important reason, though, is that the rent is too expensive. The landlord just raised it by fifty dollars, and it is just not worth it.

_____

_____

_____

_____

LANGUAGE TIPS

Signals

Signals help the reader follow your ideas from one reason to the next. These examples are from the sample compositions.

One reason I enjoy it so much is . . .
Next, . . .
Also, . . .
The most important reason that I treasure my harmonica is that . . .
First of all, . . .
Another reason I immigrated to this country is that . . .
The most important reason that I moved . . .

 **PRACTICE**

Add signals to the following composition.

My Neighbors

Lately, I have been miserable over the neighbors that moved next door   1
to my house almost six months ago. _____ they do not control their dogs. I used to have a nice garden with beautiful flowers, and I could not understand why the flowers were disappearing. One day I woke up from the sound of barking dogs, looked out the window, and saw the dogs jumping around in my garden.

_____ is that they have wild parties.   2
Almost every evening they have people over. They must have many relatives and friends. They turn the music up so loud that it almost kills my ears. Then they start shouting and dancing.

that almost every night after midnight they start fighting. A week ago someone called the police because they started yelling and arguing in front of their house. The next morning when I talked to the lady who called the cops, she told me that the husband was drunk and that he was beating his wife. Before these people moved in, my neighborhood was nice and quiet, but now the situation is intolerable. I hope they move away and leave the neighborhood the way it used to be.

Adapted from a composition by Tiopa Techiryan

PRACTICING WHAT YOU HAVE LEARNED

Put the following sentences in correct order. Write the numbers of the sentences in the outline form below. Suggestions: Underline the signals. Find the main idea and the reasons before you look for the details.

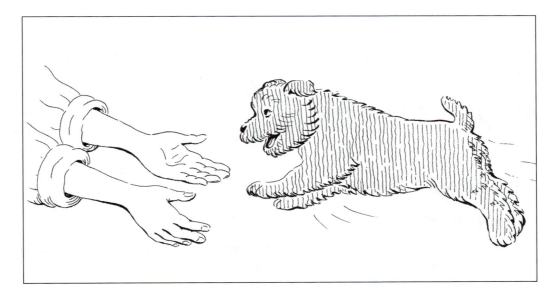

Do You Really Want a Dog?

1. No one likes it when dogs bark constantly, jump on guests, destroy property, or bite children.
2. And let's not forget the regular bath and flea control that the animal needs.
3. Another reason people grow weary of being a dog owner is that they are unprepared for the expenses.

4. They expect a calm, friendly companion, and maybe what they get is a hyperactive, temperamental monster.

5. Dog food, shots, and unexpected health problems all take a lot out of the average budget.

6. Perhaps the most important reason people change their minds about being dog owners is that they get tired of the day-to-day care.

7. People get tired of owning a dog for several reasons.

8. Second, behavior problems can turn dog owners against their pets.

9. Before falling in love with a darling puppy, people should think ahead of all the problems that owning a dog can create.

10. First of all, they are sometimes disappointed in the personality of the pet.

11. Day after day, they have to feed the dog, clean up after it, and walk it.

Main idea: _____

Reason 1 + Details: _____ _____

Reason 2 + Details: _____ _____

Reason 3 + Details: _____ _____

Reason 4 + Details: _____ _____

Conclusion: _____

YOUR TURN TO WRITE

Step 1: Preparing to Write

SELECTING A TOPIC

With your instructor's guidance, select a topic that you have a clear opinion about and you can develop with detailed reasons.

EXPLORING IDEAS THROUGH MAKING A LIST

Make a list of ideas related to your topic. As you did for the freewriting technique, allow your mind to explore, and write everything that comes to mind, without judging or censoring anything.

Do not worry about correct grammar or spelling. Do not write complete sentences. Instead, write key words, phrases, and ideas. For example, if your topic is the Getty Museum, you might write the following:

Topic: The Getty Museum

no entrance charge
beautiful paintings and statues
located in Malibu
Van Gogh's Irises
inexpensive to visit
gift shop — too small
gorgeous gardens
free parking
not far from Los Angeles
on the coast
small restaurant with
  good food and reasonable prices
you have to make a reservation
  for parking
fascinating ancient manuscripts
fussy inlaid furniture (I don't like it)

Step 2: Planning and Organizing

NUMBERING IDEAS

Look at your list of ideas and identify a main idea. Write *M* in front of the main idea. Often, you might not find the exact words you need for a main idea. In this case, write a main idea and add it to your list.

For example, the list of ideas about the Getty Museum does not include a main idea. As you know, a main idea consists of a topic and a comment. "The Getty Museum" serves as a topic, but what is the comment?

If you look more closely, you will see that most of the items on the list give good reasons for visiting the museum. Thus, the ideas on the list suggest the following as an appropriate main idea:

The Getty Museum is a wonderful place to visit.

In the example below, the main idea appears as a new item near the bottom of the list.

M   main idea
1, 2, 3   reasons: supporting points and details

```
1    no entrance charge

3    beautiful paintings and statues

2    located in Malibu

3    Van Gogh's Irises

1    inexpensive to visit

     gift shop — too small

2    gorgeous gardens

1    free parking

1    not far from Los Angeles

2    on the coast

1    small restaurant with good food
       and reasonable prices

     you have to make a reservation for parking

3    fascinating ancient manuscripts

     fussy inlaid furniture (I don't like it)

Added later:

M    The Getty Museum — wonderful

2    attractive setting

3    fantastic art collection
```

After you have a main idea, identify and number the ideas that support your main idea. These are your reasons and the details for each reason.

Each number represents one reason and the details that support it. The numbers will also guide you in putting your reasons in effective order.

You can add ideas to your list at any time. For instance, two ideas have been added to the example list. First, "2 attractive setting" gives the general idea for the details "located in Malibu," "on the coast," and "gorgeous gardens." Next, "3 fantastic art collection" gives the general idea for the details "beautiful paintings and statues," "Van Gogh's Irises," and "fascinating ancient manuscripts."

Cross out any ideas that do not support your main idea, as shown in the above list.

MAKING A ROUGH OUTLINE

Using the information on your numbered list, make a rough outline with key ideas, as shown in the sample on the opposite page.

OUTLINE

Main idea	_The Getty Museum — a wonderful place to visit_
Body	
Reason 1	_inexpensive to visit_
Details	_not far from Los Angeles_
	(low transportation cost if you live in LA)
	free parking
	no entrance charge
	small restaurant with good food and reasonable prices
Reason 2	_attractive setting_
Details	_located in Malibu_
	on the coast
	gorgeous gardens
Reason 3	_fantastic art collection_
Details	_beautiful paintings and statues_
	Van Gogh' Irises
	fascinating ancient manuscripts
Conclusion	_I recommend the Getty Museum to anyone visiting_

Use this outline as a guide.

OUTLINE

Main idea _____

Body

   Reason 1 _____

Details _____

_____

_____

_____

_____

Reason 2 _____

Details _____

_____

_____

_____

_____

Reason 3 _____

Details _____

_____

_____

_____

_____

_____

Conclusion _____

_____

Step 3: Writing the First Draft

Write your first draft. Reminder: focus on content and organization. Make sure that your reasons are clear and that you include plenty of specific supporting details.

Step 4: Revising

PRACTICE

Revise the following composition. Move details from one location to another so that they support the appropriate reason. Add details to one reason. Add one signal.

No More Big City for Many People

It is no surprise that every year many people move out of the big cities in this country. One reason that they move is that they are unhappy about the air quality. Next, they are tired of the traffic and crowds. Also, many people are fed up with the high crime rate related to drugs, car-jackings, homicides, and riots. The crime rate keeps going up, and no one feels safe in big cities anymore. Lots of people cannot find housing at a reasonable price, so they move out. Young couples cannot afford to buy their own home in large cities. Students face the toughest hardships of all because of their limited incomes. Because of this, they often have to live with a roommate or a relative. Smog covers most large cities like a large umbrella. It is unfortunate that so many people are forced to leave a city that they may think of as their home.

YOUR TURN

Review your draft for ways to revise it. You may do this by peer response and/or self-evaluation.

PEER RESPONSE

Exchange drafts with your partner. Follow the general guidelines listed on the next page.

1. Read your partner's draft twice. The second time you read it, discuss any unclear spots with your him or her.

2. Check the draft for clear organization. Refer to the Checkpoints for Revision that follows. Point out any possible problems to your partner.

3. What information or details would you like to know that your partner has not included? Tell your partner what you would like to know. Then your partner can consider adding this information.

SELF-EVALUATION

Review your own draft for ways to improve the content and organization. Refer to the Checkpoints for Revision given below.

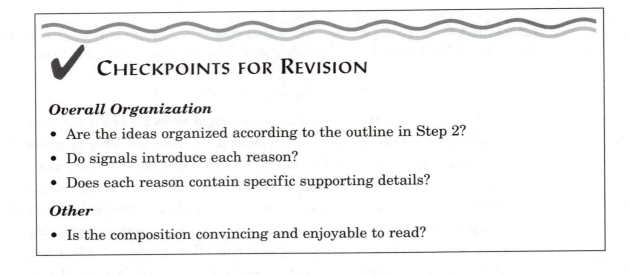

CHECKPOINTS FOR REVISION

Overall Organization

- Are the ideas organized according to the outline in Step 2?
- Do signals introduce each reason?
- Does each reason contain specific supporting details?

Other

- Is the composition convincing and enjoyable to read?

Step 5: *Proofreading and Editing*

PRACTICE

Edit the following draft. Find these errors.

	Number of Errors to Find
Spelling	1
Missing subject	1
Missing verb	1
Run-on sentence	2
Sentence fragment	2
Present or past tense	7

My Professor Frank Little

Proffessor Frank Little, my data processing instructor at Santa Monica   1
College sixteen years ago, was a wonderful teacher. To begin, he always
well-organized. He prepare his class materials carefully, and at the begining   3
of the semester he told the students what would be covered and what his class
policies were. Then he teach the class step by step. As a result, his lectures   5
were easy to follow.

Second, he had a good understanding of educational psychology.   7
I remembered one time he said that some students could not remember
numbers well. Because they were more literature-minded people. Another time   9
said that students who had special talent usually came up with their
own ideas in writing their own programs instead of following the teacher's   11
instructions. This help us develope self-confidence.

Finally, Professor Little was friendly, he was always nice to students and   13
eager to help them with their problems. One time when I am having lunch in
the cafeteria. I see him eating and helping a student with his program.   15
Sometimes he even helped students who were not in his class, he really
showed the students that he cares about their success. With all these good   17
qualities, Professor Little really impressed me and gave me the confidence to
do my best in his class.   19

Adapted from a composition by Hsi-Tai Chan

YOUR TURN

Proofread and edit your draft for grammar and visual presentation. You may do this by peer response and/or self-evaluation.

PEER RESPONSE

Exchange drafts with your partner. Read your partner's draft twice. The second time you read it, point out possible errors to your partner. Refer to Checkpoints for Proofreading and Editing, which follows.

SELF-EVALUATION

Proofread and edit your draft. Refer to Checkpoints for Proofreading and Editing, which follows.

✔ **CHECKPOINTS FOR PROOFREADING AND EDITING**

• Have you found and eliminated errors?

• List the grammatical errors that you need to proofread and edit.

_____

_____

_____

_____

_____

_____

_____

_____

Step 6: Writing the Final Draft

Write your final draft with the revisions and corrections. After you finish, proofread and edit it again carefully.

Step 7: Following Up and Evaluating Progress

SUGGESTED ACTIVITIES

Small-Group Response, Appendix 2, page 229
Traveling Compositions, Appendix 2, page 230
Responding to Your Classmates Writing, Appendix 2, page 230

BENEFITING FROM FEEDBACK

Make sure you understand your pattern of strengths and weaknesses. Continue your program of independent study. Focus on how to overcome your weaknesses.

Ideas for Writing

Write about one of the following topics.

Personal Topics

1. *The reasons for an important decision you made* (Choose one.)
   Coming to this country (or city)
   Coming to school
   Studying English
   Living in a house (apartment, with a family, or with a roommate)
   Getting married (or staying single)
   Having children (or not, or waiting to have them later)
   Buying a certain car
   Choosing a particular career path or major
   Giving up a habit
   Making a major purchase, such as a computer

2. *The reasons you enjoy a particular hobby* (Name the hobby.)

3. *The reasons you liked (or disliked) a certain teacher* (Be specific about the teacher and the situation.)

4. *The reasons you enjoyed (or did not enjoy) a specific trip or vacation* (Be specific about the trip.)

5. *The reasons you enjoy (or do not enjoy) living in the city, town, or area where you live now.* (Name the city, town, or area.)

6. *The reasons you have for convincing someone of something* (Choose one of the suggestions.):
   Giving your family good reasons for a new car
   Convincing an interviewer that you are the right person for the job
   Convincing a financial aid office that you deserve financial aid
   Convincing a university to accept you as a student
   Giving your family good reasons for the major you have selected
   Convincing your family that you need their cooperation so that you can go to school
   Convincing a friend that he or she should do something (or not do something)
   Giving your boss good reasons to let a certain employee go or to give you a promotion

7. *The reasons you like (or dislike) a certain holiday* (Name the holiday.)

8. *The reasons it is easier to live on your own (or with your parents)*

9. *The reasons your teenager should live with the family*

10. *The reasons your teenage children should not stay out late on a school night, or the reasons you should be allowed to stay out late on a school night*

11. *The reasons you like (or dislike) going shopping*

12. *The reasons you like (or dislike) a particular store, restaurant, or tourist spot.* (Name the store, restaurant, or tourist spot.)

Nonpersonal Topics

13. *The reasons that a particular tourist spot is a good (or bad) place to visit* (Name the spot.)

14. *The reasons teenagers should not get married*

15. *The reasons for a certain human behavior* (Choose one.)
    People moving out of the city where you live
    Feeling unhappy in a foreign country
    Returning to a person's native country to live
    Immigrating
    Giving up studying English
    Doing drugs
    Experiencing culture shock
    Losing a job
    Watching television
    Divorcing
    Moving out of the family house
    Getting married

16. *The reasons that certain activities or substances are good (or bad) for people* (Choose one.)
    Playing a specific sport
    Smoking
    Watching television
    Pursuing a specific hobby

17. *The reasons that living in a foreign city can be difficult*

18. *Why pets are a pleasure or a bother* (Name a specific kind of pet.)

19. *The reasons it is easier (or harder) to be an adult than to be a child*

20. *The reasons for a current political situation* (Be specific.)

21. *The reasons flexible work hours benefit everyone*

22. *The reasons people are attracted to (or reject) religion*

23. *The reasons people should be allowed to select their own marriage partner*

24. *The reasons people are prejudiced against* _____

Your Own Idea

25. If you have an idea for a topic, present it to your instructor. He or she will determine if it is appropriate for this assignment.

    Important: You need your instructor's approval before you start your assignment.

CHAPTER 5

Explaining with Parallel Points

In this chapter, you will provide parallel points to explain your main idea. *Parallel* means belonging to the same category. The list of categories is endless, but possible categories include advantages (or disadvantages), customs, minor annoyances in everyday life, things that make a person homesick, and hobbies (or favorite activities).

For each parallel point, you will give specific supporting details. Examples and reasons can serve as parallel points. They can also serve as specific supporting details for parallel points.

In your opinion, what are the advantages of being single?

Sample 1

No "Grave of Love" for Me

I have found several advantages to single life. First of all, I love the freedom to be completely spontaneous and free like a bird in the forest. I can go out when I want, make friends with anybody I want, and have fun without any interference from anybody. I can spend my money as I please, whenever I want, without feeling guilty. I can take a vacation or travel any time I feel like it.　　1

Another advantage is that the living space is all mine. When I prefer being alone, no one interrupts me asking where his socks are. No one switches the channel I'm watching on TV. No one waits at the door when I come home late. No one shares the closet with me or complains that my clothes are all over the bed.　　2

One more advantage is that I have fewer family obligations. No in-laws come to my house to tell me how to arrange my life. My Christmas gift list is short. I don't need a special calendar to remember birthdays. I don't have to cook unless I'm hungry, and I can clean the house when I'm in the mood. No one calls me at 5:30 to say, "Honey, my boss is coming over for dinner tonight."　　3

According to a common saying, "Marriage is the grave of love." Maybe it's not true, or maybe it is, but why take a chance and at the same time sacrifice all the advantages of being single?　　4

Adapted from a composition by Mei-Huey Su

1. In your opinion, which of Mei-Huey's advantages is the most convincing? Why? _____

_____

_____

2. Do you agree with her? Explain. _____

_____

_____

3. What are the advantages of being married? _____

_____

_____

_____

Do you know of any customs that seem odd to people who are not familiar with the culture that practices them?

Sample 2

Korean Customs

Several customs from my culture might seem odd to a foreigner. First, when Koreans enter the house, they take off their shoes. According to my grandmother, this is because a long time ago, our houses were very different from modern houses. In ancient Korea, people didn't sleep on raised beds, so they had to keep the floor very clean.   1

Second, in Korea some people, especially the older generation, like to eat dog meat. Most foreigners don't understand this custom. They say it's "disgusting" because "dog is man's best friend," but horses are also good friends to humans, and Europeans eat their meat. What's the difference?   2

Last, if students do something wrong, the teacher can physically punish them. It's very common and happens frequently. A few years ago an American was caned in Singapore because he painted graffiti on walls and cars. The American networks broadcast it as if it were important news. If it had happened to a Korean, it wouldn't have become big news in Korea.   3

There's no point in comparing one culture to another to determine which one is right or better. The only way to look at the differences is to learn about them and respect them.   4

Adapted from a Composition by Chris Lee

1. In your opinion, which of the customs that Chris explained is the most interesting? Why? _____

_____

2. Do you agree with Chris's conclusion? Explain. _____

_____

3. Name additional customs that might seem odd to people who are not from the same culture _____

_____

_____

_____

What minor annoyances bother you in everyday life?

Sample 3

Keep Away from Me!

1
Three things annoy me a lot in everyday life. It really bothers me when friends want me to buy things, such as cosmetics, from them. These friends are sales representatives for a company that sells at home parties. They gather as many friends as possible in their home and try to sell them their products. My closet is filled with sealed bottles of cosmetics, but it is hard to say "no" under pressure. I'm completely fed up with these parties.

2
Another annoyance for me is careless driving in this city. Some people don't even bother to put on the blinker when they change lanes, or they forget to turn it off. This habit can be dangerous. I want to yell at these drivers, "You idiots!"

3
The thing that annoys me the most is gunfire in the middle of the night in my neighborhood. A gunman (woman?) shoots to scare the raccoons and skunks from the nearby park. The first time I heard the gunshots, I was very frightened. The next morning I found out that the dog next door died from two bullets in his chest. What if a person gets shot accidentally? I'd like to tell all these people to stay away from me forever!

Adapted from a composition by Teruyo Tsuchiya

1. In your opinion, which of the annoyances that Teruyo explained is the most convincing? Why? _____

_____

_____

2. Do you have any similar annoyances? Explain.

_____

_____

_____

3. Do you have any advice for Teruyo? _____

_____

_____

Have you ever felt homesick? You probably have. What made you homesick?

Sample 4

Homesick for Indonesia

The three things I miss the most about Indonesia are the parties, my social status, and my family. Thinking about the parties in my native country really makes me homesick. When people have a party, they give an open invitation to everyone in the neighborhood to attend. They spend long, leisurely hours talking, relaxing, and laughing. 1

The next thing that I miss is the social status I used to have. I used to be a branch manager in a computer vocational training company. When I decided to move to the United States, I had to give up my position and the status that went with it. I miss the respect I used to get from my customers, the company instructors, and my students. 2

The thing I miss the most about my country is my family, especially when I recall the family birthdays we celebrated almost every month. Most of all, I have been very lonely here without my wife. I have tried to fill my time with studies and sports, but nothing stops me from thinking about her constantly. If I were a bird, I would fly to meet her, just for a second. "Just for a second, Honey, but I have to go back soon because I haven't accomplished my goals yet. You know this." 3

Writing about what I miss might relieve my homesickness for a short time, but it will never go away completely. 4

Adapted from a composition by Sofjan Hendrata

1. In your opinion, which of Sofjan's points is the most convincing? Why? _____

_____

_____

2. Do you have any similar feelings? Explain. _____

_____

_____

_____

3. Do you have any advice for Sofjan? _____

_____

_____

_____

What are the activities that you enjoy doing the most?

Sample 5

The Activities I Enjoy

The activities I enjoy the most are working in the garden, doing needle-   1
work, and making things for my grandchildren. To begin, I really enjoy
gardening because I love to take care of plants and watch them grow big
and healthy. It gives me a lot of satisfaction to look at my beautiful garden
with brightly colored flowers and sweet smells.

Another activity I love is making things with yarn and needles. When I   2
embroider, I create my own colorful designs and turn a dull piece of cloth into
a happy garden. When I finish a project, I feel a satisfying sense of accom-
plishment.

My favorite activity is doing things for my grandchildren. For example,   3
I love to cook delicious and healthy food for them. Their comments make me
feel so good: "Grandma, this is great!" or "Oh, please, I'd like some
more!" When I sew dresses for them with embroidery or patchwork and
present the outfits to them, I love to see the expressions of delight on their
little faces. One time my granddaughters put on a fashion show for the
family. I felt so proud when one of the girls, acting as announcer, described
the dresses in loving detail and said, "The designer of this very special dress
is Mrs. Jovet — my grandma!" These three activities bring me a lot of joy
and give me a sense of purpose in life.

Adapted from a composition by Luz Virginia Jovet

1. Which activity does Luz explain with the most enthusiasm? Why
   did you select this point? _____

   _____

   _____

   _____

2. For which point does Luz use the most convincing details? Explain.

   _____

   _____

   _____

   _____

LOOKING AT CONTENT AND ORGANIZATION

The Main Idea

A clear main idea includes a topic and a comment.

Topic:	Single life
Comment:	Several advantages for me

I have found several advantages to single life.

Topic:	Customs from my culture
Comment:	Three might seem odd to foreigners.

Several customs from my culture might seem odd to a foreigner.

Topic:	Indonesia
Comment:	The things I miss the most
	parties
	social status
	family

The three things I miss the most about Indonesia are the parties, my social status, and my family.

How does the third main idea differ from the others?

_____

 PRACTICE

Write main ideas for these topics.

1. Hobbies

   I have three hobbies that I enjoy whenever I have the time.

2. Goals

   _____

3. Adjusting to a new culture

   _____

4. Being married

_____

5. Having fun without spending a lot of money

_____

The Body

The body of your composition is organized into points and details. Each point gives one item of the same category. Specific supporting details follow. (As a reminder, these details may include reasons or examples.)

One common way to organize the order of the points is to put the most important or most convincing point last, as in the following example.

Cigarette Advertisements Targeted to Young People

Cigarette advertisers use several effective methods to attract children and young adults. One way they entice young people is by showing the smokers of their respective brands playing sports. This tactic suggests to young people that smoking is associated with health and vigor. Healthy young women, for example, are shown playing tennis by one manufacturer.   1

Perhaps an even more effective method of attracting young smokers is through advertisements that show sexy young people having a wonderful time in party situations. This gives the impression that smoking is fun, sexy, and associated with being attractive to the opposite sex.   2

The most seductive advertising trick of the cigarette industry, however, is the use of cartoon characters to attract children to their deadly product. The tobacco industry knows that the best way to get customers is to get young people hooked on cigarettes. It's unfortunate that so many people fall victim to such misleading advertisements.   3

It may be easier to see the organization of the composition in outline form, as shown on the next page.

OUTLINE

Main idea

Cigarette advertisers use several effective methods
to attract children and young adults.

Body
Point 1

One way they entice young people is by showing the smokers of
their respective brands playing sports.

Key words in details

association with health and vigor

healthy young women playing tennis

Point 2

Perhaps an even more effective method of attracting young
smokers is through advertisements that show sexy, young
people having a wonderful time in party situations.

Key words in details

fun, sexy, attractive to the opposite sex

Point 3

The most seductive advertising trick of the cigarette industry,
however, is the use of cartoon characters to attract children
to their deadly product.

Key words in details

get young people hooked on cigarettes

Conclusion

It's unfortunate that so many people fall victim to such
misleading advertisements.

# PRACTICE

Write the missing points for the following compositions. Include signals, and write complete sentences.

Composition A

My Three Satisfying Hobbies

I have three satisfying hobbies. *To begin, I love playing the piano.* ⟨1⟩ I especially enjoy playing gospel songs. They help me express different moods. When I feel pleased, I play light and joyful songs. When I fight with my sister, I play noisy songs ferociously and release my anger. When I am blue or disappointed about something, I play slow, heavy songs, and while I play the piano, I can think more deeply about how to solve my problem.

_____ ⟨2⟩

I particularly like programs about how animals live in nature. I learn, for example, that even little bugs try to protect themselves from their enemies and to breed to preserve their kind. These documentaries give me great admiration for nature.

_____ ⟨3⟩

My family and I like taking pictures, so I have a lot of them. When I look at photos of my friends, I smile softly and remember our happy days together. When I look at the photos of myself from my childhood, I recall that time with pleasure, and a part of me wants to return to those days. Sometimes, when I look at pictures of my mother that were taken a long time ago, I realize that she has changed a lot over the years. I become sad for her, and I decide I must treat her more kindly and love her more than ever. I love my three hobbies and I know that they will continue to bring me pleasure throughout my lifetime.

Adapted from a composition by Jiwon Kim

Composition B

New Year's Wishes

I have three wishes for this New Year. _____ 1
_____ When I was in Japan, I used to
be skinny. I've been in this country for a year and a half now, and I've
gained about fifteen pounds. Since I discovered Hog 'n' Dash Ice cream,
I've been eating it too often, and I need to cut down! Also, I don't get the
exercise I used to get in Japan. I probably need to walk more, instead of
relying on cars so much.

_____ 2
_____

I'm taking two ESL classes: Writing is especially important to
me, because I want to become a bilingual secretary. I have trouble with
grammar when I write, so I need to study harder to eliminate these
problems.

_____ 3
_____

I've been married for four years, and I'm twenty-nine years old. I think it's
time to have a baby. Unfortunately, I had a miscarriage last September, but
this loss made me want to have a baby all the more. I hope to become a
mother during this new year. Maybe, by the end of this year, you'll find
a skinny, but pregnant, hardworking Japanese student sitting in class
with you.

Adapted from a composition by Sachi Ishii

Composition C

My Three Main Goals

I have three main goals. _____ 1
_____

Several of my friends have degrees, and they tell me that if I want a better
future, I need to work hard and get a degree. I don't want to be like one of
my neighbors who has been looking for a job for several months. She is not

qualified for anything more than a minimum-wage position.

_____ 2

After I get my degree, I want to look for a new job or ask for a promotion in my present job. Eventually, I will earn more money and be able to afford to buy my own house.

_____ 3

I met a person from Spain a year ago, and he told me about a lot of interesting places, such as the Alhambra, Toledo, and the Museo del Prado. Also, I want to experience the culture and the customs. Maybe I'll even see the running of the bulls in Pamplona. I'm really thinking a lot about this trip. In five years, I plan to have a degree, a better job, a house, and a round-trip ticket for Spain in my hand.

Adapted from a composition by Claudia Ortiz

The Conclusion

The conclusion ties together the entire composition. In a conclusion you can give a short summary of your points, a reference to the future, or express a final thought that grows out of the body. Often, a conclusion contains more than one of the above.

With your classmates, discuss why the following student sample conclusions are effective.

1. According to a common saying, "Marriage is the grave of love." Maybe it's not true, or maybe it is, but why take a chance and sacrifice all the advantages of being single?

2. There's no point in comparing one culture to another to determine which one is right or better. The only way to look at the differences is to learn about them and respect them.

3. I'd like to tell all these people to stay away from me forever!

4. Writing about what I miss might relieve my homesickness for a short time, but it will never go away completely.

5. These three activities bring me a lot of joy and give me a sense of purpose in life.

6. Maybe, by the end of this year, you'll find a skinny, but pregnant, hardworking Japanese student sitting in class with you!

Write conclusions for these compositions.

Composition A

Procedures in Egyptian Classrooms

Instructors and students follow several procedures in Egyptian classrooms. When the teacher arrives, all the students in the room must stand up. They may not sit down until they are told to do so. When students address their teachers, they must do so very carefully. They must never interrupt, and they must use very polite forms of speech when they talk to a teacher. Also, when the teacher gives an assignment, and a student does not turn it in when it's due, the student is punished physically and directed to complete the assignment right away. In this way, the student will never forget the lesson.

1

_____

_____

_____

2

Adapted from a composition by Ayman Mansour

Composition B

My Pet Peeves

Some annoyances really make me hit the ceiling. The first thing that bothers me is noisy gum chewing. As soon as I hear a person chewing gum loudly, my whole attention is captured. All I can hear are the sounds "tak tak chop...tak tak chop," and I can see in my mind the large mouth of a hippo chewing vigorously.

1

My second pet peeve is noisy, rushing ambulances. They have given me anxiety attacks ever since I had two unpleasant experiences with ambulances. Four years ago, an ambulance came to the house for my father, who had a serious kidney disease. The sound sickened me, as the ambulance rushed away with my father. When I had a car accident a few years ago, I heard that terrible sound again, but this time it was rushing to get me. The sound of a siren brings back these bad memories.

2

The last thing that upsets me is an unexpected phone call, especially 3
when someone is calling me to talk about something like merchandise, a
donation, or schools. The first time I got one of these calls, the person was
very friendly. I was trying to understand what he was saying, and I was
worrying that my English wasn't good. My English is still not good enough
to understand a native speaker's fast speech, so I still don't like getting these
calls.

_____ 4

_____

_____

_____

Adapted from a composition by Il Park

LANGUAGE TIPS

Signals

The student samples use signals to introduce each new point.

First of all, . . .
Another advantage is . . .
One more advantage is . . .

First, . . .
Second, . . .
Last, . . .

Another annoyance for me is . . .
The thing that annoys me the most is . . .

The next thing that I miss is . . .
The thing I miss the most about my country is . . .

To begin, . . .
Another activity I love is . . .
My favorite activity is . . .

Note: A signal for the first point is not always necessary.

PRACTICE

Fill in the missing signals in the following student composition.

My Goals for the Future

I have three main goals. _____ is   1
to open my own day care business. Right now I'm a baby-sitter in my home,
but I want to open a location outside my home. Once I get set up, I want to
take care of several children up to the age of three. I like taking care of
small kids because this stage is really beautiful. I love them very much.

_____ is to speak and write   2
English very well. This is important to me because I've chosen to live in the
United States, where English is the major language. If I want to be
successful in my day care business and feel more comfortable conversing
with people, I have to speak English better than I do now.

_____ is the one I hold closest to   3
my heart. I want to be married and have children. Ever since I was a child,
family was the most important thing in my life. Now as an adult, I would
like to have my own family and my own children. Of course, I also want to
have a good husband who will share my life's joys and sorrows. I pray to
God to help me achieve these three very important goals for my future.

Adapted from a composition by Teresa Poteranska

PRACTICING WHAT YOU HAVE LEARNED

Put the following sentences in correct order. Write the numbers of the sentences in the outline form below. Suggestions: Underline the signals. Find the main idea and the points before you look for the details.

Too Much Noise for Me

1. Another thing that annoys me is alarms — both car alarms and house alarms.
2. The noise in my neighborhood really bothers me.
3. I need to move to a new neighborhood or invest in a good set of earplugs.
4. My next door neighbor has two very nervous dogs that spend all day alone in the yard.
5. The "boom boom boom" slams right into my house, and my floor feels like it's jumping in time to the beat.
6. For one thing, the teenage boy across the street plays his heavy metal music too loud.
7. The thing that bothers me the most, though, is barking dogs.
8. They go off frequently on my street, and often they continue ringing for a long time.
9. One day a house alarm continued screaming for well over an hour. It gave me a headache.
10. He turns the volume way up, especially the bass, and opens his front door wide.
11. Everything makes those two dogs bark, and my nervous system jumps with their every piercing bark.

Main idea: _____

Point 1 + Details: _____ _____

Point 2 + Details: _____ _____

Point 3 + Details: _____ _____

Conclusion: _____

YOUR TURN TO WRITE

Step 1: *Preparing to Write*

SELECTING A TOPIC

With your instructor's guidance, select a topic that you are familiar with and that you can develop with points and details.

EXPLORING IDEAS

Listing or Freewriting. In order to develop ideas about your topic, make a list of ideas or freewrite.

Discussing Your Topic with Others. With a partner or in a small group, take turns telling about your topic.

Step 2: *Planning and Organizing*

MAKING A ROUGH OUTLINE

Make a rough outline with key ideas in effective order. Use the sample outline format on the opposite page as a guide.

Step 3: *Writing the First Draft*

Write your first draft. Make sure that your points are clear and that you have included specific, supporting details.

Step 4: *Revising*

 **PRACTICE**

Revise the following composition. Add details in two places, add one signal to introduce a new point, and write a conclusion.

My Three Main Goals

I have three main goals for the next five years. First of all, I want to   1
finish my education. In the past, I was a student at the University of
Guadalajara for a year. I loved the university atmosphere because it gave me
a sense of purpose. Even though taking ESL classes now will slow me down
a little, I am committed to my goal.

I plan to support my kids in their education. They need my careful guidance because they don't seem to have a clear idea of what they want to do and accomplish in the future. My oldest son, for example, is confused. He is searching, and I want to do my best to help him, if only by providing him with a positive example of someone who attends college to learn and grow.

1

My last main goal is to keep my family together. I have seen families fall apart because everyone becomes so involved in their own lives that they forget about the rest of the family. My dream for my family is that after my kids get married, we can still all live together in the same building, as several separate families that belong to one big family.

2

Adapted by a composition by Manuel Garcia

OUTLINE

Main idea _____

_____

Body
  Point 1 _____

_____

Details _____

_____

Point 2 _____

_____

Details _____

_____

Point 3 _____

_____

Details _____

_____

Conclusion _____

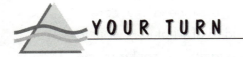

YOUR TURN

Review your draft to revise it. You may do this by peer response and/or self-evaluation.

PEER RESPONSE

Exchange compositions with your partner. Follow these general guidelines:

1. Read your partner's draft twice. The second time you read it, discuss any unclear spots with him or her.
2. Check the draft for clear organization. Refer to the Checkpoints for Revision that follows. Point out any possible problems to your partner.
3. What information or details would you like to know that your partner has not included? Tell your partner what you would like to know. Then your partner can consider adding this information.

SELF-EVALUATION

Review your own draft for ways to improve the content and organization. Refer to the Checkpoints for Revision that follows.

✔ CHECKPOINTS FOR REVISION

Overall Organization

- Are the ideas organized according to the outline in Step 2?
- Do signals introduce each point?
- Does each point contain specific supporting details?

Other

- Is the composition convincing and enjoyable to read?

Step 5: Proofreading and Editing

PRACTICE

Edit the following draft. Find these errors.

	Number of Errors to Find
Spelling	2
Missing subject	1
Missing verb	1
Run-on sentence	2
Sentence fragment	2
Present or past tense	2

Many Thanks

I'm grateful for many things in my life. First, I'm ~~greatful~~ *grateful* for a nice   1
American lady that I met at a senior center in Chicago. When I first moved
to Chicago, I am very lonely, so I decided to help at the senior center. Millie   3
was the manager, she welcomed me and put me to work as a volunteer. At
first, was hard to understand the people there, but Millie was so kind and   5
patient, she gave me the confidence that I can get used to speaking with
native speakers and be usefull in this country.   7

Next, I grateful for a kind friend in Los Angeles: Atsuko. She has a lot
of friends here and knows a lot about this area. She introduced me to many   9
nice people and gave me a lot of information about the city. Throught her,
I made many friends and adjusted to the city easily.   11

What I'm the most grateful for is my husband's work transfer to the United
States. It's so important to learn about other countries and cultures. I   13
especially like having the opportunity to study here. Even if I am a foreigner
and older than many of the other students. Also, I don't have to be a full-time   15
student in order to take classes. It is satisfying for me to continue learning and
growing. My favorite words in English are "thank you." Because these words   17
express what I want to say to so many people.

Adapted from a composition by Teruyo Tsuchiya

YOUR TURN

Proofread and edit your draft for grammar and visual presentation. You may do this by peer response and/or self-evaluation.

PEER RESPONSE

Exchange drafts with your partner. Read your partner's draft twice. The second time you read it, point out possible errors to him or her. Refer to Checkpoints for Proofreading and Editing on the next page.

SELF-EVALUATION

Proofread and edit your own draft. Refer to Checkpoints for Proofreading and Editing on the next page.

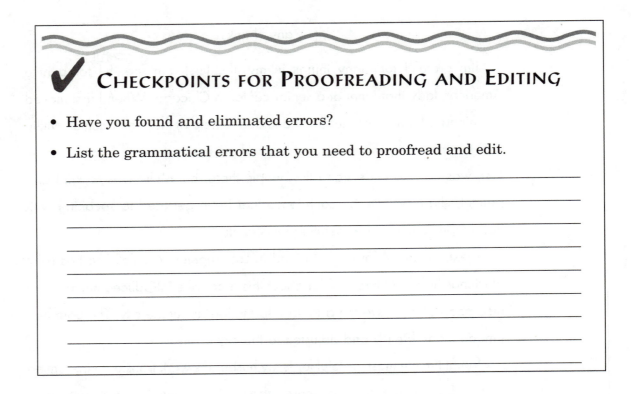

CHECKPOINTS FOR PROOFREADING AND EDITING

- Have you found and eliminated errors?
- List the grammatical errors that you need to proofread and edit.

_____

_____

_____

_____

_____

_____

_____

_____

_____

Step 6: Writing the Final Draft

Write your final draft with the revisions and corrections. After you finish, proofread and edit it again carefully.

Step 7: Following Up and Evaluating Progress

SUGGESTED ACTIVITIES

Small-Group Response, Appendix 2, page 229
Traveling Compositions, Appendix 2, page 230
Responding to Your Classmates' Writing, Appendix 2, page 230

BENEFITING FROM FEEDBACK

Make sure that you understand your pattern of strengths and weaknesses. Continue your independent study. Focus on how to overcome your weaknesses.

Ideas for Writing

Write about one of the following topics.

Personal Topics

1. *Your goals or wishes for the future.* For example: education, job/career, home/family, health, time use, and so forth.

2. *Your hobbies or favorite activities*

3. *Games or pastimes you enjoyed as a child*

4. *What you miss (or don't miss at all) about a place where you used to live*

5. *Communication problems (or successes) you've had in a new culture*

6. *Time wasters in your life*

7. *Your pet peeves* (things that bother or annoy you in everyday life)

8. *The stresses in your life*

9. *Changes you have made in your life in the last few years*

10. *The three possessions you would save in case of a fire at home, and why you would select them*

11. *Three things you are especially grateful for*

12. *The ways you procrastinate when you don't want to do something*

Nonpersonal Topics

13. *The adjustments that people have to make when they move to a new country.* (language, housing, food, social customs, school system, dating customs, and so forth)

14. *The advantages of being married / single*

15. *Ways parents can help their children do better in school*

16. *Ways married couples can improve communication*

17. *Ways people can save money on a limited budget*

18. *Bad health habits of teenagers (or other group of people)*

19. *Ways to lose weight (or to improve health)*

20. *Ways to help a person you love quit smoking*

21. *Ways to help a person you love develop a healthier life style*

22. *Ways to have fun without spending a lot of money*

23. *The benefits of a particular hobby or a sport*

24. *Ways to beat depression*

25. *Ways to stay comfortable in hot weather*

26. *The characteristics of an ideal wife / husband / partner*

27. *The characteristics of an ideal friend, teacher, doctor, salesperson, or other*

28. *The benefits of computers in modern-day living* (An alternative: The negative side effects of computers in modern-day living)

29. *What many people may not know about a non-English speaking culture*

30. *The difficulties of being a student*

31. *The qualities of a good marriage or committed partnership*

32. *Common worries for people in your age group*

33. *Common stresses of living in a big city*

34. *The advantages (or disadvantages) of being a woman (or a man)*

35. *The benefits of flexible working hours*

36. *The benefits of being a child (or adult)*

37. *The benefits (or drawbacks) of religion or other belief system*

38. *Specific ways people procrastinate in order to avoid doing something they don't want to do.* For example: studying for a test.

39. *Ways to enjoy the December holidays*

40. *The advantages / disadvantages of living in the city / country*

Your Own Idea

41. If you have an idea for a topic, present it to your instructor. He or she will determine if it is appropriate for this assignment.

    Important: You need your instructor's approval before you start your assignment.

SECTION TWO

COMPOSING: RESPONDING TO OUTSIDE SOURCES

CHAPTER 6

Proverbs and Quotations

In this chapter, you will choose a proverb or a quotation and write a composition based on your selection. Your composition will consist of two main parts. In the first part, you will explain briefly what you think the proverb or quotation means. In the second part, you will write a response, that is, you will express your personal reaction or opinion related to the meaning of the proverb or quotation: Do you agree or disagree with it? You can illustrate your response with examples from your own experience.

Do you believe that people who visit or live in a culture that is different from their own should follow the customs of the new culture? Should they practice their own customs instead?

Sample 1

An Exception

The saying "When in Rome, do as the Romans do" (St. Ambrose) means that wherever you go, you should follow the customs of the people who live there. Often this is true, but there are exceptions. For example, when I came to the United States, I didn't know very much about the customs here. I did know one custom, though. I knew that people here are used to keeping their shoes on in the house.   1

One day I was invited to the house of my father's American friend. It was the time for me to use my only knowledge about Americans' habits. As soon as the door opened and I took my first step to enter the house, I felt strange because I entered the house with my shoes on. Soon after that, my father's friend said very politely, "Could you please take off your shoes?" I was surprised, but soon I understood. My father's friend was wearing slippers inside the house. Quickly, I took off my shoes and changed to slippers.

2

When we were having dinner, I told my father's friend that I thought Americans wore shoes in their houses. He told me that he had lived in Japan for several years and that he liked the Japanese custom of wearing slippers in the house. Because of his preference, he adopted the Japanese custom in America. From this experience I learned that "doing as the Romans do" is good advice most of the time, but one must also be ready for any exceptions.

3

Adapted from a composition by Takejiro Hirayama

1. In one sentence, what is Takejiro's opinion?

_____

_____

2. Have you had any similar experiences? Explain.

_____

_____

Can you always save time by hurrying?

Sample 2

Haste Makes Waste

The English proverb "Haste makes waste" means that if people perform a task rapidly, they will do it carelessly and have to do it over again correctly. In my experience, this saying is very true. Last month I bought a Vitamaster exercise bicycle with a triple-action movement. It came in a big box, and I had to put it together. I was excited, and I wanted to try out my new exercise bicycle as soon as possible, so I hastily started to assemble it without first reading the instructions. After I finished assembling the Vitamaster, it didn't work properly. I had to take it apart and read the instructions carefully. When I understood the instructions clearly, I started to assemble the exerciser all over again. Now it works smoothly and properly.

1

Due to my haste and carelessness, though, I wasted too much time assembling the Vitamaster the first time. Based on this experience, I'll try to take the time I need for any important task in the future because "haste makes waste."

Adapted from a composition by Thuong Phung

1. In one sentence, what is Thuong's opinion?

   _____

   _____

2. Have you had any similar experiences? Explain.

   _____

   _____

LOOKING AT CONTENT AND ORGANIZATION

The Main Idea

A clear main idea for the assignment in this chapter includes the following:

The proverb or quotation:	Haste makes waste.
The source:	a proverb
The meaning:	If people perform a task rapidly, they will do it carelessly and have to do it over again correctly.

The English proverb "Haste makes waste" means that if people perform a task rapidly, they will do it carelessly and have to do it over again correctly.

The Body

The body of your composition consists of your response. Do you agree with the proverb or quotation? Explain why or why not. You may give one detailed example, several short examples, reasons, or you may use another method of organizing your ideas.

In my experience, this saying is true. Last month I bought a Vitamaster exercise bicycle with a triple-action movement. It came in a big box, and I had to put it together.... (See Sample 2.)

Which method did Thuong use to organize his response?

The Conclusion

As noted in previous chapters, the conclusion ties together the entire composition.

> Based on this experience, I'll try to take the time I need for any important task in the future because "haste makes waste."

What lesson did Thuong learn from his experience?

_____

YOUR TURN TO WRITE

Step 1: Preparing to Write

SELECTING A TOPIC

Select a proverb or quotation whose meaning you know.

EXPLORING IDEAS

Clustering. In the center of a sheet of paper, write the proverb or quotation, and draw a circle around it. Next, allow your mind to come up with ideas freely; accept any idea that is related in any way. Write these ideas in positions around the proverb or quotation. Circle each new idea, and draw a line to connect it with the proverb or quotation.

Continue in the same manner with additional ideas. Connect each new idea with the one before it. In this way, one idea will lead to another, and you will end up with a page of ideas that branch out from the proverb or quotation.

After you have produced a full page of ideas, select one branch or several related branches to focus on in your composition.

The example of clustering on the next page is based on the proverb "Haste makes waste."

Step 2: Planning and Organizing

Write a rough outline with key ideas. Use the outline on page 119 as a guide.

Step 3: Writing the First Draft

Write your first draft. Focus on content and organization, and worry about grammar later.

Step 4: Revising

Review your draft and revise it. Select one or both of these methods: peer response or self-evaluation.

Step 5: *Proofreading and Editing*

Proofread and edit your draft. Choose one or both of these methods: peer response or self-evaluation.

Step 6: *Writing the Final Draft*

Write your final draft with the revisions and corrections.

Step 7: *Following Up and Evaluating Progress*

SUGGESTED ACTIVITIES

Small-Group Response, Appendix 2, page 229
Traveling Compositions, Appendix 2, page 230
Responding to Your Classmates' Writing, Appendix 2, page 230

BENEFITING FROM FEEDBACK

Continue your independent study. Focus on how to overcome your weaknesses.

OUTLINE

Main idea

    The proverb
    or quotation: _____

    The source: _____

    The meaning: _____

    _____

Body

    Your response — Do you agree?
    Why or why not?

    Explain _____

    _____

    _____

    _____

    _____

    _____

    _____

    _____

    _____

    _____

    _____

Conclusion _____

    _____

    _____

    _____

Ideas for Writing

ASSIGNMENT 1

Discuss the following proverbs or quotations with your classmates. Then, select one and write a composition based on your choice.

Proverbs

1. The love of money is the root of all evil.
2. Don't count your chickens before they hatch.
3. A friend in need is a friend indeed.
4. Haste makes waste.
5. Where there's a will there's a way.
6. Two heads are better than one.
7. You can't judge a book by its cover.
8. It's better to be safe than sorry.
9. Out of sight, out of mind.
10. Absence makes the heart grow fonder.
11. Money can't buy happiness.

As a result of class discussion, add to the list of proverbs:

12. _____

_____

13. _____

_____

14. _____

_____

Quotations

1. When in Rome, do as the Romans do. (St. Ambrose)
2. There's no place like home. (J. Howard Payne)
3. A man's true wealth is the good he does in this world. (Mohammed)

4. Maybe this world is another planet's hell. (Aldous Huxley)
5. The weak can never forgive. Forgiveness is the attribute of the strong. (Mahatma Gandhi)
6. You must do the thing you think you cannot do. (Eleanor Roosevelt)
7. Mistakes are part of the dues one pays for a full life. (Sophia Loren)
8. The most popular labor-saving device is still money. (Phyllis George)

ASSIGNMENT 2

Find a book in the library that contains proverbs or quotations. Select one and write a composition based on your choice.

ASSIGNMENT 3

Select a proverb or quotation from a language other than English. Translate it into English, and write a composition explaining its meaning. Provide plenty of details and examples.

CHAPTER 7

Writing a Summary

In this chapter, you will practice writing summaries. This will prepare you for the summary and response writing assignments in Chapter 8.

The sample selections here are followed by summaries.

Selection 1

One at a Time

A friend of ours was walking down a deserted Mexican beach at sunset. As he walked along, he saw another man in the distance. As he grew nearer, he noticed that the local native kept leaning down, picking something up, and throwing it into the water. Time and again he kept hurling things into the ocean.   1

As our friend approached even closer, he realized that the man was picking up starfish that had been washed up on the beach and, one at a time, he was throwing them back into the water.   2

Our friend was puzzled. He approached the man and said, "Good evening, friend. I was wondering what you are doing."   3

"I'm throwing these starfish back into the ocean. You see, it's low tide right now, and all of these starfish have been washed up on to the shore. If I don't throw them back into the sea, they'll die up here from lack of oxygen." 4

"I understand," my friend replied, "but there must be thousands of starfish on this beach. You can't possibly get to all of them. There are simply too many. Don't you realize this is probably happening on hundreds of beaches all up and down this coast? Don't you see that you can't possibly make a difference?" 5

The local native smiled, bent down, and picked up yet another starfish. As he threw it back into the sea, he replied, "Made a difference to that one!" 6

Sample Summary 1

"One at a Time" by Jack Canfield and Mark V. Hansen, from their book *Chicken Soup for the Soul*, tells the story of a man who wanted to make the world a better place. The man was on a beach in Mexico, throwing live starfish back into the ocean. A second man approached him and said that there were too many starfish to toss back, so throwing only some of them back wouldn't make any difference. As the first man tossed another starfish back into the water, he pointed out that it made a difference to the one he had just tossed back.

In this story, which person's opinion do you agree with? Why?

_____

_____

Selection 2
Hyperhigh[†] Tech

"Hey! Look at this! Now they make devices that you can attach to your plumbing to program the amount of water you use when you take a shower!"

That's my husband Walt talking. He has just laid down the newspaper he was reading, and his sincerity and enthusiasm are increasing with every word he speaks. I know that look on his face. He doesn't even see me anymore. He has totally missed the strange look on my face because he has focused his entire attention on this computer-on-a-showerhead. 1

2

"What about hands and faucets?" I protest. "Why aren't hands and faucets good enough to get the basic job done?"

3

[†]excessively high

"Oh," he responds with a wide and knowing smile. "With this device , you can actually measure the water you use, and you can set various times for various temperatures." I can tell he thinks I should be really impressed.

4

Now the darn thing sounds like one of those horrible pay showers in camping grounds in Europe, the ones that always shut off at the wrong time or turn freezing cold when your time is over.

5

I repeat my question: "What's the matter with hands and faucets? No computer chips to burn out. Always reliable. No error messages that we can't find in the manual, and completely adjustable to however you want your water."

6

Now he has that look on his face that says, "Why are you so simple-minded? Why can't you just appreciate how technology makes our lives so much better?!"

7

We turn away from each other, lapsing into a cold silence for several minutes. A five-minute internal stew.[†]

8

I make stew in my good, old, faithful, fifteen-year-old crock-pot. Walt would rather use a fancy new kitchen gadget that measures the temperature to the nth-degree and regulates the timing, on and off, accurately to a nanosecond. His crock-pot would go on and off all day at a variety of preset times. Same old stew in the end, though!

9

We've got two VCRs. The first VCR does a fine job, but it has only nine buttons. Then we bought the second VCR. It has twenty-three buttons and can do really amazing things, according to Walt. I imagine that we could even hook it up to our phone machine and control the movie volume from as far away as Alaska.

10

Of course, we've never tried it. In fact, we have to study the manual each time we want to do anything fancier than play and rewind.

11

Then it happened. The motor in the second VCR (the fancy one) gave out, and the repair estimate came to $170. "A new VCR is not all that much more," Walt argued. I know what he *really* meant: Higher tech VCRs have come out since we got our last one.

12

Well, maybe he is right. The next VCR might be able to control the bathroom plumbing and the crock-pot — all by remote!

13

† stew — (1) quiet anger; (2) a mixture of meat and vegetables

Sample Summary 2

In "Hyperhigh Tech" by Ann Strauch, the author describes her husband Walt's enthusiasm for computerized devices and her own doubts about the value of "high tech" gadgets. She gives three examples. In the first example, Walt expresses great enthusiasm over a computerized showerhead. The author argues that hands and faucets do the same job just as well or better. In the next example, the author argues that an old fashioned crock-pot makes the "same old stew" that a computerized crock-pot makes. In the last example, Walt wants to get a new VCR, one with all the up-to-date technology, but the author argues that a fancy VCR performs unnecessary functions and makes day-to-day functions too complicated.

What is your opinion about "high tech" gadgets?

_____

_____

LOOKING AT CONTENT AND ORGANIZATION

The Main Idea

A clear main idea includes the following:

The title:	"One at a Time"
The author(s):	Mark V. Hansen and Jack Canfield
The source (if applicable):	*Chicken Soup for the Soul*
The main idea:	Story of a man who wanted to make the world a better place.

"One at a Time" by Jack Canfield and Mark V. Hansen, from their book Chicken Soup for the Soul, tells the story of a man who wanted to make the world a better place.

The Summary

A *summary* is a brief explanation of the main ideas of a piece of writing. Summaries leave out most of the details and include only what is absolutely necessary. The purpose of the summary is to inform the reader about the main ideas of the work, using your own words.

When you write a summary, follow these guidelines.

WRITING A SUMMARY

1. Keep the summary as short as possible.
2. For the most part, use your own words. If you quote exact words from the original, use quotation marks.
3. Leave out nonessential details.
4. Do not give your own opinions.

To decide if an idea is essential ask yourself "Is this idea general or specific?" Often, general ideas are essential, and specific, supporting details are not. (See Part 1, page 170 for practice with general versus specific ideas.) However, there are no strict rules to guide you in deciding if an idea is essential or nonessential.

Identifying essential ideas is a skill that calls for a measure of judgment, and your judgment will develop through practice.

YOUR TURN TO WRITE

Step 1: Preparing to Write

SELECTING A TOPIC

Select and read a short story or an article. Photocopy your selection and turn it in with your composition. After reading your selection, identify the main ideas and tell them to a classmate or another person.

Step 2: Planning and Organizing

Write a rough outline with key ideas. Use the outline format on the opposite page as a guide.

Step 3: Writing the First Draft

Write your first draft.

Step 4: Revising

Review your draft and revise it. Select one or both of these methods: peer response or self-evaluation.

OUTLINE

Main idea of the composition

    The title: _____

    The author(s): _____

    The source:
    (if applicable) _____

    The main idea
    of the source: _____

_____

_____

Body

    Summary of the
    essential ideas: _____

_____

_____

_____

_____

_____

_____

_____

_____

_____

_____

_____

_____

_____

Step 5: *Proofreading and Editing*

Proofread and edit your draft. Choose one or both of the following methods: peer response or self-evaluation.

Step 6: *Writing the Final Draft*

Write your final draft.

Step 7: *Following Up and Evaluating Progress*

SUGGESTED ACTIVITIES

Small-Group Response, Appendix 2, page 229
Traveling Compositions, Appendix 2, page 230
Responding to Your Classmates' Writing, Appendix 2, page 230

BENEFITING FROM FEEDBACK

Continue your independent study. Focus on how to overcome your weaknesses.

 PRACTICE

This practice will prepare you for the summary and response compositions that follow in Chapter 8.

Select one of the sample summaries in this chapter, and write a response to it. Do you agree with the author's main idea? Why or why not? Explain your opinion in detail. Write a conclusion at the end.

CHAPTER *8*

Articles from Magazines and Newspapers

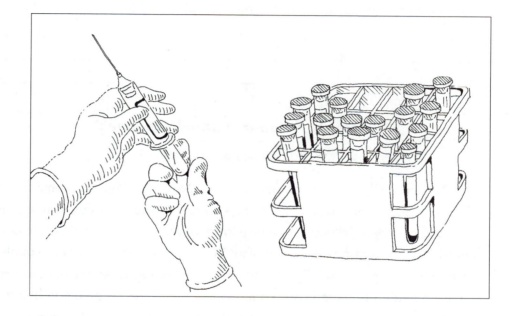

In this chapter, you will select and read an article from a newspaper or magazine and prepare a summary and response based on your selection.

Sample Summary and Response 1

Making a Profit at the Expense of Public Health

The article "AIDS Scare Shakes Germany" in *News for You* (November   1
17, 1993) is about a company in Koblenz, Germany, that caused a health
panic. In order to cut costs, the company didn't test all its blood products for
AIDS, and then it sold all the blood to hospitals throughout Germany
and Europe. The article continues to explain how officials responded to this
emergency and the difficulties they had encountered.

I don't agree with this company's business practices because now   2
thousands of Germans and other Europeans are afraid that they may have
gotten the AIDS virus from the company's bad blood products all because
this company conducted its business improperly. Why did the company

think only of its own selfish interests? Why didn't the officials think about others? Didn't they think about all the unhappiness they were causing? Suppose they had gotten the AIDS virus? How would they feel? Also, what about the rest of society? Caring for people with AIDS can cost the public a lot of money. I felt very unhappy when I read this article. This news is bad for everyone. The company is now closed, but not before doing harm to a lot of innocent people.

Adapted from a composition by Khanh Nguyen

Do you agree or disagree with Khanh's opinions? Explain.

_____

_____

_____

Sample Summary and Response 2

Good Science or Bad Ethics?

"Scientist Clones Human Embryos" in *News for You* (November 10, 1993) reports that scientists know how to create two embryos from one in a lab. Dr. Robert Stillman at Georgetown University was the first to create twins in vitro, and now he hopes that this new technique will help couples with infertility problems. This brings up the question of ethics because an embryo might be treated as a commodity, rather than as a human being.   1

In my opinion, this is an unfortunate situation because it decreases the value of a human being. If people can choose babies the same way they can choose dolls in department stores, then they may think of a baby as a possession, such as a car, a house, or a TV set. People have to love, care for, and be thankful for their babies for who they are. They have to appreciate their uniqueness, which they can't do if they can simply order a copy of a frozen embryo. Babies who are less smart or less beautiful than others are still valuable and worthy human beings, especially because of their uniqueness. For these reasons, I want this new technology to be controlled and not offered widely to the public.   2

Adapted from a composition by Mee-Hyang Song

Do you agree or disagree with Mee-Hyang's opinions? Explain.

_____

_____

_____

Sample Summary and Response 3

The True Victims of Smoking

"Smoking Parents Lose in Court" in *News for You* (December 1, 1993)   1
tells about a court decision to protect a minor against exposure to secondhand
smoke. Elyse Tanner has asthma, and her parents' smoking has caused many
health problems for the girl. When the case went to court, the judge ruled
against the parents and Elyse's grandmother got custody of her.

I agree with the court's decision because children should not be exposed   2
to cigarettes in their homes. One reason is that children follow their parents'
example. If the parents smoke, then in the future, the children will also smoke.
Next, secondhand smoke is harmful for everyone, especially for children. A
government expert, who is mentioned in the article, said that secondhand
smoke can cause ear problems, lung damage, and asthma in children. Most
important of all, however, is that it seems obvious that the parents in this case
are not interested in what is best for their child. How can they not know that
their smoking is harmful to their asthmatic daughter? It seems obvious to me that
the parents are neglecting their child. I'm very happy that the judge ruled
against the parents in this case. It is not fair for children to suffer from health
problems because of their parents' bad habits.

Adapted from a composition by Shahzedi Memon

Do you agree or disagree with Shahzedi's opinions? Explain.

_____

_____

Sample Summary and Response 4

Tolerance and Table Manners

"In Be Appreciative, Act like a Pig" (*Los Angeles Times*, October 10,   1
1994), Norine Dresser shows how multicultural differences in table
manners can cause misunderstandings. Dresser gives an example of a man
from the Philippines named Peter who is a guest in the home of
his new American friends the Gordons. The problem arises when Peter
belches at the end of his meal. The Americans think he is acting like a pig,
but Dresser explains that Peter is simply complimenting the good food. The
point is that table manners are different from culture to culture.

I believe that both sides, Peter and the Gordons, missed important   2
points. On the one hand, the Gordons knew that their guest was from a
different culture, so they should have expected some differences in table
manners. On the other hand, Peter should have considered that he was

in a new culture, and he should have acted more prudently. In any case, in cross-cultural situations, people need to remember to be more tolerant and more prudent. In this way they can avoid feeling uncomfortable because of cultural differences.

Adapted from a composition by Esteban Andiola

Do you agree or disagree with Esteban's opinions? Explain.

_____

_____

LOOKING AT CONTENT AND ORGANIZATION

The Main idea

A clear main idea includes the following:

The title of the article:	"Scientist Clones Human Embryos"
The source:	*News for You* (November 10, 1993)
Main idea:	Scientists know how to create two embryos from one in a lab.

"Scientist Clones Human Embryos" in *News for You* (November 10, 1993) reports that scientists know how to create two embryos from one in a lab.

The Body

The body of your composition consists of a summary and your response. Do you agree with the ideas in the article? In your response, explain why or why not. Reread Sample Summary and Response 2.

Summary:	Dr. Robert Stillman at Georgetown University was the first ...
Response:	In my opinion, this is an unfortunate situation because ...

The Conclusion

The conclusion ties together the ideas of the entire composition.

Conclusion:	For these reasons, I want this new technology to be controlled and not offered widely to the public.

YOUR TURN TO WRITE

Step 1: Preparing to Write

Select a short magazine or newspaper article. Photocopy it and turn it in later with your composition. After you have read the article, prepare for the next step using one or more of the following methods: making a list of ideas, freewriting, clustering, or sharing ideas with a classmate or other person.

Step 2: Planning and Organizing

Make a rough outline with key ideas. Use the following outline format as a guide.

```
                            OUTLINE

Main idea of the composition

    The title of
    the article:          _____

    The source:           _____

    The main idea
    of the article:       _____

                          _____

Body
    Summary
    and response          _____

                          _____

                          _____

                          _____

                          _____

                          _____

                          _____

                          _____

Conclusion                _____

                          _____
```

Step 3: Writing the First Draft

Write your first draft using your outline. Focus on content and organization, and worry about grammar later.

Step 4: Revising

Review your draft and revise it. Use on or both of the following methods: peer response or self-evaluation.

Step 5: Proofreading and Editing

Proofread and edit your draft. Select one or both of the following methods: peer response or self-evaluation.

Step 6: Writing the Final Draft

Write your final draft with the revisions and corrections.

Step 7: Following Up and Evaluating Progress

SUGGESTED ACTIVITIES

Small-Group Response, Appendix 2, page 229
Traveling Compositions, Appendix 2, page 230
Responding to Your Classmates' Writing, Appendix 2, page 230

BENEFITING FROM FEEDBACK

Continue your independent study. Focus on how to overcome your weaknesses.

Ideas for Writing

ASSIGNMENT 1

Read the following newspaper article, and write a summary and response based on it.

CULTURE SHOCK RESULT OF MANY SMALL THINGS

Warwhoop, April 20-27, 1989
El Camino College
Torrance, California

By Jose Tingson
Staff Writer

1   When nursing student Yogi Patel attended high school in Dallas, the first thing that shocked* her was the sight of pregnant teenagers and students smoking.

2   Patel and her family came to the United States in 1983, after living for seven years in England, where teenage pregnancy and smoking are a rarity.

3   "The young people here have so much freedom: they can pretty much do what they want. But, the teenagers in England are very conservative* and always stick to the rules,*" Patel said.

4   Patel's observations are typical of what every foreign student goes through, trying to adapt to* a new culture and environment that are usually far different from where he or she came from.

Older students surprising

5   Patel was also surprised to see older people going back to school to acquire a high school diploma or taking college courses for enjoyment.

6   "In England, you don't see people over fifty taking high school courses or college classes. But it's different here; it's normal and, in fact, admirable for older persons to go back to school," Patel said.

7   "In England," Patel added, "going to a pizza restaurant is comparable to dining in an exquisite* French restaurant, where a jacket and tie are required.

8   Here it would be a bit strange if you did so; casual* attire would do," Patel said with a smile.

Learning to drive

9   For Steve Ch'ng, who came to California a year ago from Singapore and is currently majoring in industrial engineering, there were different aspects* of the American culture which he had to adjust to.

10   The first thing he had to learn was how to drive properly here.

11   "In Singapore, everybody drives in the left lane. It took me about two weeks to get used to driving in the right lane," Ch'ng said.

12   Since Singapore enjoys one of the lowest crime rates in the world, where the death penalty* is given to those who are caught selling drugs or owning a gun illegally, Ch'ng doesn't feel comfortable about the high crime rate in Southern California.

13   "Because I don't feel too safe walking or going out at night, I have to think twice before doing so. Almost every night the news reports on TV show gang* killings and drive-by shootings," Ch'ng said.

Longs for fresh air

14   Another aspect of Southern California which troubles Ch'ng is the ever-present smog in Los Angeles.

15   "It's a big adjustment for me because I come

* Words and phrases marked by an asterisk are defined in the glossaries following the readings.

from a country where you can breathe fresh air pretty much all the time and then go to a whole new environment where the air quality is not too good," Ch'ng said.

16   Unlike Patel and Ch'ng, Ichiro Mochizuki still has a difficult time expressing himself clearly because of the language barrier.*

17   When Mochizuki came here four years ago from Japan, he could hardly speak conversational English. And although the business management major has improved his English quite a bit,* he still has difficulties.

18   According to David Jordan, adviser to the International Students Club, communication is a major problem faced by foreign students.

19   "Because of the language problem, it's very hard for me to get along* with other people," Mochizuki said.

GLOSSARY

to adapt to	to get used to
aspect	part
barrier	something that blocks something else
casual	informal
conservative	strict, not liberal
exquisite	fancy, elegant
gang	group that meets in the streets (usually young people who may get in trouble with the police)
to get along	to have a comfortable relationship
penalty	punishment
quite a bit	a lot
to shock	to surprise
to stick to the rules	to follow the rules

 ASSIGNMENT 2

Select and read a newspaper or magazine article and write a summary and response based on your choice. When you turn in your composition, include a copy of the article.

 ASSIGNMENT 3

Select an advice column from a newspaper (or other source) and write a summary and response based on it. In the response section, give your advice. When you turn in your composition, include a copy of the advice column.

CHAPTER 9

Selections from Literature

In this chapter, you will read an excerpt from a short story or a folk tale and write a summary and response based on it.

The first group of selections consists of excerpts from literature, followed by sample compositions based on these excerpts.

Selection 1

The following selection is an excerpt from Orlando Romero's short story "Nubes." (*Nubes* — Spanish = Clouds) In this selection, the narrator and his mother are anguishing over their abandonment by the narrator's father. The mother expresses her thoughts first.

> "How am I so wrong for him? He drinks and drinks. I don't make him   1
> happy. He finds no peace here at home. I wonder how he's doing in
> California? Six months now, not a word. Doesn't he realize he's my only

man? No one kisses my breasts, no one talks to me in the lateness of the evenings, no man makes me laugh like he does. That first year, it was so fine, so rich and gentle. What distracted* him? Why can't he raise himself above it, instead of drinking himself below it?"

In her longing* glances* and the warmth of our fire, I wonder where my father is. My memories of him are mixed between the good and the confused. No one takes me fishing up to the beaver* ponds now, or lets me shoot the twenty-two.* I wonder what California is like? Why doesn't he send me a pocketknife or a yo-yo,* like he said he would?

2

GLOSSARY

beaver	water animal
to distract (someone)	to divert someone's attention
glance	quick look
longing	full of great desire
twenty-two	a type of gun
yo-yo	toy

Sample Summary and Response 1

Anguish

The excerpt from Orlando Romero's "Nubes" describes the anguish that a woman and her son experience. The wife misses her husband terribly. For example, she recalls his kisses and the laughter she shared with him. She remembers how good it was when they were together, as in the statement, "That first year, it was so fine, so rich and gentle." She's a good wife. She has been faithful. Tragically, though, she blames herself for her husband's long absence. She says, "I don't make him happy."

1

The next person affected by the father's absence is the son. His feelings are mixed — good memories together with the pain of losing his father. He misses doing things with his father, and he can't understand why his father doesn't send any evidence of his love for him, such as the knife or toy he promised he would send.

2

The third person suffering is the father. Even though his feelings are not described in this excerpt, one can only guess how he feels. He went to California to find a better job, but didn't succeed as he hoped he would. He probably thinks he has failed his family. He is ashamed and feels defeated, and to ease his pain, he has turned to alcohol for comfort.

3

As I see it, he probably loves his wife and son very much, but has avoided them out of shame and self-blame. I wish I could tell that father to set his feelings of shame aside and return to the loving arms of his family.

4

What is your opinion about the people in "Nubes?"

_____

_____

_____

Selection 2

The following excerpt is from the short story "Doña Toña of Nineteenth Street" by Louie the Foot González. The story is set in Sacramento, in a Spanish speaking neighborhood. The narrator, a young boy, gives his initial impressions of Doña Toña, the local *curandera*, an old woman who uses faith and herbs to cure people of their illnesses.

Her name was Doña Toña and I can't help but remember the fear I had of the old lady. Maybe it was the way all the younger kids talked about her:

1

"Ya, man. I saw her out one night and she was pulling some weeds near the railroad tracks and her cat was meowing away* like it was ready to fight that big black dog and, man, she looked just like a witch. Like the Llorona* was trying to dig up her children."

2

"Martín's telling everybody that she was dancin' aroun' real slow and singin' some witch songs in her backyard when it was dark and everybody was asleep."

3

Doña Toña was always walking somewhere…anywhere…even when she had no particular place to go. When she walked, it was as though she were making a great effort because her leg was kind of funny. It dragged a little and made her look as if her foot were made of solid metal.

4

Her face was the color of lightly creamed coffee. The wrinkles around her forehead and eyes were like the rings of a very old tree. They gave her age as being somewhere around seventy-five, but as I was to discover later, she was really eighty-nine. Even though her eyes attracted much attention, they always gave way to her mouth. Most of the people that I had observed looking at her directed their gaze* at her mouth. Doña Toña had only one tooth to her name and it was the strangest tooth I had ever seen. It was exceptionally long and it stuck out from her upper gum at a forty-five degree angle. What made it even stranger was that it was also twisted.* She at one time probably had an overabundance* of teeth, until they began to push

5

against each other, twisting themselves, until she had only one last tooth left. It was the toughest of them all, the king of the hill, 'el mero chingón.'*

GLOSSARY

el mero chingón	"Dangerous" (Spanish vulgar term meaning the strongest, most powerful of all)
gaze	look
Llorona	from Mexican folklore, a tragic woman who lost her children
to meow away	to continue making the sound of a cat
overabundance	more than a person needs
to be twisted	to be turned around

Sample Summary and Response 2

Fear, Humor, and Memories

"Doña Toña of Nineteenth Street" by Louie the Foot González is about a young boy's fear of an old woman in his neighborhood. One reason he feared her is that the other kids told him scary stories. They referred to her as a witch, and they described her doing odd things at night. Another reason Doña Toña terrified the boy is that she looked so frightening. For example, her mouth was particularly ugly.   1

I really enjoyed the details the author used to describe the old woman's mouth and her remaining last tooth: "It was the toughest of them all, the king of the hill, 'el mero chingón.'" This sentence reinforced the color, impact, and humor in the frightful sight of Doña Toña's mouth.   2

I can sympathize with kids who fear very old and unusual people. I remember having a similar experience. When I was very young, my family lived a block from an old woman. She lived in a house that looked (to me) like it was haunted. My older sister told me the old woman was a witch, and I felt terrified if this old lady even looked at me through her window. Reading about Doña Toña brought back this childhood memory for me and made me laugh about it.   3

Do you have any similar memories about older people from childhood? Explain. _____

_____

_____

Supplementary Summaries and Responses

Sample 3

The following summary and response is based on a short story from *More Surprises* by Burton Goodman (Jamestown Publishers, Providence, Rhode Island, 1990).

Pete Hopkins's Talents

In Edward D. Hoch's short story "A Deal in Diamonds," the main character Pete Hopkins, a professional thief, has personal characteristics that could serve him well in an honest profession. First, Pete has a good imagination that helps him develop a brilliant idea for a robbery. When he observes a fountain under the window of a jewelry store, he figures out that stolen diamonds could easily be hidden in the fountain for a short time.   1

Second, Pete has good planning skills. He is able to plan the robbery carefully, step by step, from setting up a fake "customer" for the diamonds, to distracting the salespeople, to tossing the diamonds out the window into the fountain, and coming back for them later. The plan is so clever that it almost guarantees success.   2

Last, this enterprising thief also has well-developed persuasive skills. Even though his friend Johnny Stoop thinks the plan is crazy at first, Pete is successful at motivating Johnny to help him carry out the plan. It's unfortunate that Pete wastes his talents in illegal activities when he could use them well in a legitimate profession.   3

Sample 4

The following summary and response is based on a short story from *More Surprises* by Burton Goodman (Jamestown Publishers, Providence, Rhode Island, 1990).

The Future: A Computer with Emotions?

The story "Key Item" by Isaac Asimov is about a team of scientists trying to find out why a computer is not working. Because this is an important computer, it must be fixed soon, but nobody can come up with the solution. After the scientists argue about it for a while, one of them figures out the problem: The computer wants the scientists to include "please" in their commands to it. Once they say "please," the computer starts working perfectly.   1

I think Asimov wants to say that computers are becoming so advanced 2
that one day humans will lose the ability to control them. Of course, no one
can know the future, but I think it's fascinating to imagine that computers
can eventually become so "smart." Maybe this could happen because
computers can store a lot of information, and they can perform many
functions that are amazingly humanlike. Who knows? Maybe one day they'll
be able to think and feel like humans. In any case, the story has given me
something to think about.

Adapted from a composition by Virginia Macías

The two examples that follow are based on a short story from *Short Takes in
Fiction* edited by Saitz and Steiglitz (Addison Wesley, Reading, Massachusetts,
1993). They demonstrate different responses to the same source.

Sample 5

Death and God

"An Appointment in Samarra" by Somerset Maugham tells about a 1
servant in Baghdad who tries to run away from Death. In this story, Death
appears as a person who bumps into the servant in the marketplace.
The terrified servant escapes to Samarra. Later, the master sees Death in the
marketplace, and Death tells the master that he was surprised to
see the servant in Baghdad, because he had an appointment with him
that night in Samarra.

The story shows Maugham's belief in fate. The servant can't escape 2
from Death, even though he has tried his best. I agree with the author's idea
that our lives are in the hands of forces beyond our control, because I
believe that my life is controlled by God.

The following are examples of how my life is not under my control. When I drive on the highway, I don't know if I will have an accident, because I can't control the other drivers. Also, if I fly to Mexico next month, something could happen that would affect my trip. I could get sick, or the airlines could go on strike. Last, I have no idea how many years I will live. I take care of my health, but that's no guarantee of a long life. In reality, so many things are completely out of one's control.

I also enjoyed the humor in the story because of the surprise ending and because of the imaginary figure of Death. Even though Death is just a creative touch to the story, the idea of fate, or God, as the controller of our lives is absolutely real.

Adapted from a composition by Rosa Maria Aguilar

Sample 6

Fate or Free Will?

Somerset Maugham's "An Appointment in Samarra" is a story about one man's fate. A servant frantically tries to avoid his time of death, but he unknowingly sends himself to his own death.

Obviously, the author believes in fate — that everyone has his or her own predetermined destiny. I do not agree with this. On the contrary, I believe in free will, as my life's experiences demonstrate. In 1954 my family moved from North to South Vietnam, because we disagreed with the Communist regime. We did not accept a fate controlled by communist thought. Unfortunately, in 1975 South Vietnam fell to the Communists. I was forced into a reeducation camp; my family was poorly treated. Even this sad time of our lives did not convince us to accept a fate we didn't believe in. So, in 1979, my family escaped to the United States. I followed them later, and we reunited in 1991. In this country, we have more favorable opportunities in business and education. We successfully changed our fate.

Another reason I believe that we can control our fate is that scientific research has helped humankind to prevent or cure several dangerous illnesses such as cancer, heart disease, polio, the plague, and cholera. In the past, people with these diseases had to accept their fate and await death. Now, they have a choice about their health and their future. Somerset Maugham's story is entertaining because of the ironic ending, but I don't believe in fate at all. I decide my own future.

Adapted from a composition by Thuong Phung

LOOKING AT CONTENT AND ORGANIZATION

The Main Idea

A clear main idea includes the following:

The name of the selection:	An excerpt from "Nubes"
The author:	Orlando Romero
The main idea:	The anguish that a woman and her son experience in the absence of their husband and father

> The excerpt from Orlando Romero's "Nubes" describes the anguish that a woman and her son experience in the absence of their husband and father.

The Body

The body of your composition consists of a summary and your response.

Summary:	The wife misses her husband terribly. For example, . . .
Response:	She is a good wife. She has been faithful. Tragically, though, . . .

Note: Sometimes a summary and a response are clearly separated, with the entire summary appearing before the response, as in Sample Summary and Response 2. Other summary and responses, however, mix the summary and response together, as in Sample Summary and Response 1.

The Conclusion

The conclusion ties together the ideas in the entire composition.

Conclusion:	I wish I could tell that father to set his feelings of shame aside and return to the loving arms of his family.

YOUR TURN TO WRITE

Step 1: Preparing to Write

Choose a selection from literature. If it's a selection not included in this text, photocopy it and turn it in later with your composition. After you have read the selection, prepare for the next step using one of the following methods: making a list of ideas, freewriting, clustering, or sharing ideas with a classmate or other person.

Step 2: Planning and Organizing

Make a rough outline with key ideas. Use the outline format below as a guide.

OUTLINE

Main idea of the composition

The title of
the selection: _____

The author: _____

The main idea
of the selection: _____

_____

Body
Summary and
response: _____

_____

_____

_____

_____

_____

_____

_____

Conclusion _____

_____

Step 3: Writing the First Draft

Write your first draft.

Step 4: Revising

Review your draft for ways to revise it. Select on or both of the following methods: peer response or self-evaluation.

Step 5: Proofreading and Editing

Proofread and edit your draft. Choose one or both of the following methods: peer response or self-evaluation.

Step 6: Writing the Final Draft

Write your final draft with the revisions and corrections.

Step 7: Following Up and Evaluating Progress

SUGGESTED ACTIVITIES

Small-Group Response, Appendix 2, page 229
Traveling Compositions, Appendix 2, page 230
Responding to Your Classmates' Writing, Appendix 2, page 230

BENEFITING FROM FEEDBACK

Continue your independent study. Focus on how to overcome your weaknesses.

Ideas for Writing

ASSIGNMENT 1

The following selection is from "Shizuko's Daughter" by Kyoko Mori (Fawcett Juniper, NY, 1993). The scene takes place in Masa's garden. Yuki, Masa's granddaughter, is visiting during a summer vacation from college. Masa wants to discuss Yuki's future with her.

Masa walked slowly toward the house, stopping now and then to snip off   1
dead leaves or fading flowers, pull out the weeds growing between the plants.
There were few weeds. The drought* had killed those that had sprung* up
after Yuki's visit. Yuki had spent hours of her two-week visit weeding the flower
beds and vegetable plots. Masa wondered if Yuki had spent so much of her
time outside because she wanted to avoid talking to her.

But Yuki must have been anxious to see us, Masa told herself. She had visited in the last weeks of June, as soon as her college was out for the summer. She said she wanted to stay longer but couldn't because she had to work. Besides, she needed to use the studio at her college for photography and she had to go to the library to read. 2

"Why do you have to read books or even go to college to study art?" Masa had asked her. "I thought you would be able to learn just from doing it on your own.* Isn't that how all the great artists learned? They didn't go to college." 3

Yuki shook her head. "That was a different time, and a lot of them were apprenticed* to other artists even then. They didn't just teach themselves everything. It's hard to explain." 4

"I was thinking you could live with us all year round and still be an artist. This is a nice quiet place to live. Why not?" 5

"I don't know. How would I support myself here?" 6

"You wouldn't have to worry about that. Grandpa's pension* is enough for all three of us if we live modestly.* If you want to work, you can always give lessons." 7

"But I don't want to spend a long time looking at kids' drawings." 8

"You can coach the track team at the village school. Even people around here read about you in the papers last year when you won those competitions."

"I don't want to coach* track* teams." 9

"What will you do after you graduate, anyway? Will you become a teacher somewhere else then?" 10

"Grandma, I don't know." Yuki sighed. "I just started college. I don't know what I'll do afterward." 11

"What is the use of going to college if you don't know what you're going there for?" 12

"Maybe I'm going *because* I don't know. I just want to study art now. I have no idea about four years from now or even next year. I don't want to think that far ahead." 13

Masa was going to point out that this was too haphazard* a way to live when Yuki abruptly* stood up and put on her straw hat. 14

"I'm going to the garden. I didn't weed your petunia patch yet," she said. "Let me know if there's something else I can do." 15

Yuki was never rude or irritable on this visit. Even when they disagreed, 16
her face was always full of patience. But something was wrong. Masa felt a
strain* when they talked, and she was sure that Yuki felt it also.

GLOSSARY

abruptly	suddenly
to be apprenticed	to be a helper for and student of an expert in some skill (a common way to learn a skill in the past)
to coach	to instruct (often a sports team)
drought	long dry spell of weather with little or no rain
haphazard	without a plan, not organized
modestly	not expensively
on one's own	alone
pension	income for a retired person
to spring (sprang, sprung)	to shoot up; to grow
strain	feeling of discomfort between people
track	running as a sport

 Discussion Questions

Discuss the following questions in small groups. Your instructor may ask you to write down your answers. For number six, write your own question for discussion.

1. What are Masa's concerns? What does she want from Yuki? Why? Explain.

2. What are Yuki's concerns? What does she want from Masa? Why? Explain.

3. In the last paragraph, what does "the strain" refer to?

4. Which point of view — Masa's or Yuki's — do you agree with more? Why? Explain.

5. Are your reasons for being in school similar to or different from Yuki's? Explain.

6. _____

_____

The following selection is from *April and the Dragon Lady* by Lensey Namioka. The novel is set in the United States and focuses on the relationship between April and her Chinese grandmother. In this scene, April is taking her grandmother to see the doctor. This is her grandmother's first visit to a doctor in the United States.

I gave Grandma's name to the receptionist, and we were told to take a seat in the waiting room. The magazines there were all old, and in any case, Grandma wouldn't read magazines in English. 1

A young nurse came out into the waiting room. "May? Is May here?" she asked, looking around the room. 2

When nobody answered, she looked at the card in her hand. "My?" she tried. 3

Still no one responded. The nurse's glance* came to Grandma. "Are you May? Or My? Er... maybe I'm not pronouncing your name right." 4

"My grandmother's name is Mei-yun Chen. Is she the one you're looking for?" 5

The nurse smiled with relief.* "She sure is. So I got it right the first time." 6
She looked down at Grandma. "Come on in with me, May."

I remembered the respectful way everybody addressed Grandma at her 7
birthday party: Grandma Chen or Auntie Chen by the younger generations,
and Mrs. Chen by those of her own generation. Only very close friends, like
Mrs. Liang, were allowed to call her Mei-yun. Even though Grandma
was acting funny lately, she was still entitled* to her dignity.* It seemed
disrespectful for this young nurse to address Grandma by her first name and
to get it wrong, too.

"My grandmother's given name is not May," I said firmly to the nurse. 8
"It's Mei-yun. But please call her Mrs. Chen."

The nurse continued to smile brightly. "I know you people have your 9
own customs, but it's our policy here to use first names. We feel more
comfortable with that."

The condescending* way she talked really grated* on me. " You may 10
feel more comfortable with first names, but how do your patients feel?"

I was talking to air. The nurse was already leading Grandma down the 11
corridor.* Fuming,* I got up and followed. At the door to the doctor's office,
the nurse asked me to wait outside. "While your grandmother is seeing
Dr. Wilton, can you fill out these forms for us? We need some information
since this is her first visit.

I looked at Grandma's face, which seemed to be showing signs 12
of panic. "I think I should go inside with her," I said. "My grandmother
doesn't speak much English."

"That's all right," the nurse assured me. "She doesn't need to." 13

Before I could say another word, the door to the doctor's office shut in my 14
face. I took the forms the nurse gave me and sat down on a chair in the
waiting room. I knew immediately that I couldn't answer half the questions on
the sheet. For a start, I didn't know her maiden name* or how many
siblings* she had. Nor did I have a clue* about her medical history.

I finally decided to fill in the answers that I knew and then ask Grandma 15
about the rest. Just as I was putting away my ballpoint pen, the nurse came
out and rushed up to me. "Can you come with me? We're having a little
trouble with your grandmother."

"What's the matter?" I asked, as we hurried to the examination room. 16

"The only thing she'll let us do is take her blood pressure," said the 17
nurse. "But she won't get undressed! Dr. Wilton can't examine her unless
she gets undressed!"

GLOSSARY

clue	hint, idea
condescending	treating someone with an air of superiority
corridor	hallway
dignity	self-respect
to be entitled	to deserve something, to have the right to something
to fume	to be very angry
glance	look
to grate on someone	to bother / to irritate someone
maiden name	family name before marriage, often changed when a woman marries in a Western culture
relief	escape from discomfort
sibling	brother or sister

 ### Discussion Questions

Discuss the following questions in small groups. Your instructor may ask you to write down your answers. For number eight, write your own question for discussion.

1. Why is April angry? Explain your answer in detail.

2. How does April's grandmother feel? Why? Explain your answer in detail.

3. How are April's and her grandmother's expectations different from the nurse's and doctor's expectations? Be specific. Who is right? Explain your answer in detail.

4. How is the medical system in Western cultures different from the medical systems in other cultures? (Focus your answer on a medical system you're familiar with.)

5. How are customs regarding names and addressing people different in various cultures? (Focus on two specific cultures.)

6. How are attitudes toward older people different among various cultures? (Focus on two specific cultures.)

7. Have you had any experiences similar to the one described in this excerpt? Explain.

8. _____

_____

ASSIGNMENT 3

This excerpt is from the short story "Another Evening at the Club" by Alifa Rifaat in *Stories from the Rest of the World*, edited by Scott Walker (The Graywolf Short Fiction Series, Graywolf Press, St. Paul, 1989). It is a flashback to an earlier scene. In it a young woman is meeting her husband-to-be for the first time.

Note: You may not know all of the vocabulary in this passage, and not all of these words appear in the glossary. You do not need to know the meaning of every word. Do not use your dictionary while you are reading.

It was only a few years ago that she had first laid eyes on him at her 1
father's house, meeting his gaze that weighed up her beauty and priced it
before offering the dowry.* She had noted his eyes ranging over her as she
presented him with the coffee in Japanese cups that were kept safely locked
away in the cupboard for important guests. Her mother had herself laid
them out on the silver-plated tray with its elaborately embroidered spread.
When the two men had taken their coffee, her father had looked up at her
with a smile and had told her to sit down, and she had seated herself on
the sofa facing them, drawing* the end of her dress over her knees and
looking through lowered lids at the man who might choose her as his wife.
She had been glad to see that he was tall, well-built and clean-shaven
except for a thin greying moustache. In particular she noticed the well-cut
coat of English tweed and the silk shirt with gold links.* She had felt herself
blushing* as she saw him returning her gaze. Then the man turned to her
father and took out a gold case and offered him a cigarette.

"You really shouldn't, my dear sir," said her father, patting his chest with 2
his left hand and extracting a cigarette with trembling* fingers. Before he
could bring out his box of matches Abboud Bey had produced his lighter.

"No, after you, my dear sir," said her father in embarrassment. Mingled* 3
with her sense of excitement at this man who gave out such an air of worldly
self-confidence was a guilty shame at her father's inadequacy.*

After lighting her father's cigarette Abboud Bey sat back, crossing his 4
legs, and took out a cigarette for himself. He tapped it against the case
before putting it in the corner of his mouth and lighting it, then blew out
circles of smoke that followed each other across the room.

"It's a great honour for us, my son," said her father, smiling first at Abboud 5
Bey, then at his daughter, at which Abboud Bey looked across at her and
asked:

"And the beautiful little girl's still at secondary school?" 6

She lowered her head modestly* and her father had answered: 7

"As from today she'll be staying at home in readiness for your happy life together, Allah* permitting," and at a glance from her father she had hurried off to join her mother in the kitchen.

"You're a lucky girl," her mother had told her. "He's a real find.* Any 8 girl would be happy to have him. He's an Inspector of Irrigation though he's not yet forty. He earns a big salary and gets a fully furnished government house wherever he's posted, which will save us the expense of setting up a house — and I don't have to tell you what our situation is — and that's besides the house he owns in Alexandria where you'll be spending your holidays."

GLOSSARY

Allah	God (in Islam)
to blush	to turn red in the face with embarrassment
dowry	money paid to the groom by the bride's family
to draw	to pull
inadequacy	the condition of not being good enough
links	jewelry worn on shirt cuffs
to mingle	to mix
modestly	with humility
real find	desirable husband-to-be
to tremble	to shake from fear or nervousness

 Discussion Questions

Discuss the following questions in small groups. Your instructor may ask you to write down your answers. For number six, write your own question for discussion.

1. How do the girl's parents feel about this marriage? Why? Be specific. Give evidence from the story.

2. How does Abboud Bey feel about this marriage? Draw evidence from the story, and use your imagination.

3. How does the girl feel about this marriage? Draw evidence from the story, and use your imagination.

4. What's your personal opinion about this marriage?

5. In general, what's a good way for a person to select a marriage partner?

6. _____

_____

The following selection is from *Paradise of the Blind* by Duong Thu Huong. The novel is set in Russia and Vietnam. In this passage, the author gives views of various people leaving on trips. The first scene takes place in Russia; two lovers are parting in a train station. The second scene takes place in Vietnam; the narrator is watching refugees eager to leave from the Noi Bai Airport. The narrator also describes her own thoughts as she waits for her airplane to leave.

Note: You may not know all of the vocabulary in this passage, and not all of these words appear in the glossary. You do not need to know the meaning of every word to understand what is going on in the story. Do not use your dictionary while you are reading.

I bit into the peach, its sugary juice filling my mouth. Sweet enough to wake the dead. Out the window, I saw passengers rushing toward the train. On the platform, a couple were embracing.* A farewell kiss. The woman was teary. Separation, this ancient pain, perhaps the greatest of all human sadnesses.   **1**

The young man on the platform tossed his bundle over his shoulder. She hugged him one last time. Their straw-colored hair mingled,* their heads glowing under the lamplight like two silkworm cocoons.* A final kiss and they separated. The young woman cast a tall, thin shadow across the cement platform. The man's voice echoed from the window of one of the cars. The woman waved and then started to walk. After about ten steps, she turned around, her face streaming with tears. The train started up. The man's voice was drowned in the wind.   **2**

I watched the woman left behind on the platform until the train station blurred* behind us. The train streaked* through the suburbs,* plunging* into a landscape of endless, rolling hills. In the half-light of dusk, I could just make out their dark masses of green.   **3**

Good-bye. A train whistle, like a cry …   **4**

No separation could rival* the vulgarity* of those in my country, at the Noi Bai Airport. The day I left, only one person, lost in a village somewhere beyond the river, cried for me. I thought of Aunt Tam, of her broken heart, as I watched the young people on the platform.

The Noi Bai Airport. It all came back to me: the swarms of people, the suffocating* heat. Even worse was the anxiety, the fear that tormented these people as they went through the customs formalities. Their numbed,*   **5** panicky* faces, their hair clammy with sweat, their eyes furtive, darting about impatiently, ferreting everywhere, ready for a last-minute disaster.

Outside, on the other side of a black iron grill, was another crowd, just as anxious, just as sweaty and frightened. These were the parents and friends of those departing. They all waited for deliverance.* When all the customs procedures had been completed, when the crowd of travelers had passed through the last security booths and were walking toward the tarmac*, you could see, on the faces of those left behind, the relief, the joy, the pride of vicarious* success. The vision of a happier future elsewhere, anywhere but here. Smiles of contentment, faces radiant with happiness. Nowhere else in the world does separation bear the hideous* face of joy. This was a grotesque* face, a deviation* from all the rules of human nature. 6

I was alone in the middle of the line of people waiting their turn at customs. I wiped the sweat from my temples, peering* over the top of the iron gate. My mother was in the hospital, Aunt Tam was angry with me, so she wouldn't be there. I knew this, but I still looked for her in the crowd. I looked without hoping. I knew that she was crying alone, in her big, empty house on the other side of the river. 7

GLOSSARY

to blur	to become unclear visually
cocoon	"home" of a butterfly or moth before it becomes mature
deliverance	release from a bad situation
deviation	departure, separation
to embrace	to hug
grotesque	very ugly, twisted into unnatural shapes
hideous	very ugly, hard to look at
to mingle	to mix together
numbed	without sensation
panicky	extremely worried, afraid of danger
to peer	to look curiously
to plunge	to dive into
to rival	to compete with
to streak	to go so fast that it's hard to see
suburbs	neighborhoods next to the city
to suffocate	to cause someone to have trouble breathing
tarmac	airplane runway
vicarious	experienced imaginatively or sympathetically
vulgarity	ugliness, indecency

Discussion Questions

Discuss the following questions in small groups. Your instructor may ask you to write down your answers. For number three, write your own question for discussion.

1. This excerpt describes three points of view about leaving on a trip. Describe the circumstances of each and the feelings of the people involved.

2. Have you had any similar experiences when you left on a trip? Explain.

3. _____

_____

ASSIGNMENT 5

The following excerpt is from the short story "Sister Katherine" by David Nava Monreal. It tells about a school boy named Arturo and his teacher, Sister Katherine. At the beginning of the passage, Arturo is in the schoolyard, running to class a few minutes late, and he's terrified of being punished by Sister Katherine. Arturo's classmate Tony arrives in class shortly after Arturo does.

Note: You may not know all of the vocabulary in this passage, and not all of these words appear in the glossary. You do not need to know the meaning of every word to understand the story. Do not use your dictionary while you are reading.

He [Arturo] was panting* and his heart was drumming in his chest. Looking up he saw that the schoolyard was almost empty. Wobbling* up the concrete steps, he entered Sister Katherine's classroom. All the students were sitting at their desks; Arturo sat down as Sister Katherine was chalking up the morning's lesson.   1

Sister Katherine was big; her back was broad and her hips ballooned beneath her black skirt. When she turned around, the rosary* she had strung about her neck clicked, jingled, then sent a spark of light into Arturo's eyes. She scanned* the class; when she saw that Tony's desk was empty, an ugly scowl appeared on her face. She stood with her arms cradled on her breasts, not saying a word.   2

Arturo shivered;* a stream of sweat ran down his chin, then plopped on the desktop. He wondered if Sister Katherine had seen him come in late. He tried to open the book sitting before him, but his hands were shaking too much.   3

"Is there anyone missing today, class?" Sister Katherine boomed.*   4

Everyone in the class craned their necks; their eyes fell on the empty desk.   5

"Tony García!" They replied.   6

"How many times is it this week?"   7

"Three times!"   8

Sister Katherine's eyes churned* with venom.* "He has no respect for   9
learning or God!" Color came to her pallid face. "He will be punished this
time, I promise you."

The class grew silent, so silent that Arturo knew that his heart was   10
pounding loud enough to be heard. He squirmed* in his seat when Sister
Katherine turned her eyes on him. She knows, she knows that I was late but
she's not going to do anything about it.

Tony walked in smiling, he passed the threshold,* then stood in front   11
of Sister Katherine. He stood there with one leg cocked* and both hands
dangling* rudely from his pants pockets. Swaying* arrogantly,* he spoke
with words edged with defiance.*

"I guess I'm late."   12

A dark cloud passed over Sister Katherine's face, "Yes, you are."   13

Tony shrugged* his shoulders.

"And why are you late?"   14

Tony shot a glance* at Arturo, "Because I don't give a damn* about this   15
class."

In a blur Sister Katherine's hand rose into the air then came down with   16
brutal* force across Tony's mouth. It rose again and came down with even
more force; it came down again and again — the whacking sounds of the
slaps filled the classroom, and every child witnessing the beating felt a deep
fear wash over his heart. They watched as Sister Katherine's hand drew
blood from inside Tony's mouth; Tony was in shock, then without even a
whimper* tears began to roll down his cheeks. Sister Katherine slapped him
until his knees buckled and he fell helplessly to the floor.

She stood above him, her face hardened, more impenetrable* than   17
granite.* She grabbed Tony by the scuff of the neck, hauled him to his
feet, then stared straight into his eyes. "Don't ever talk to me that way! Now
that God has taught you a lesson!"

She then shoved him down the aisle and Tony staggered to his desk   18
weeping.* Arturo felt panic spread through his body, noticing that Sister
Katherine had her hands doubled up into fists. *Never, never will I disobey,
Sister Katherine, God believe me.*

GLOSSARY

arrogant	with an attitude of superiority
to boom	to make a loud noise
brutal	vicious, violent
to churn	to move vigorously or violently in a circular motion
to cock	to bend
to give a damn	rude expression
to dangle	to hang loosely
defiance	challenge, lack of respect
glance	look
granite	rock
impenetrable	not affected by (an action)
to pant	to breathe heavily
rosary	prayer beads
to scan	to look everywhere quickly for information
to shiver	to shake from fear or cold
to shrug	to move one's shoulders upwards, to indicate a lack of concern
to squirm	to move uncomfortably
to sway	to move back and forth
threshold	boundary between inside and outside
venom	poison
to weep	to cry from deep hurt
whimper	quiet crying sound
to wobble	to walk weakly, unsteadily

Discussion Questions

Discuss the following questions in small groups. Your instructor may ask you to write down your answers. For number nine, write your own question for discussion.

1. What's your opinion about Tony's behavior?

2. What's your opinion about Sister Katherine's response to Tony's behavior?

3. What effect do you believe Sister Katherine's punishment had on Tony?

4. How do you think the punishment affected Arturo and the rest of the students?

5. If you were Sister Katherine, what kind of punishment would you give Tony?

6. Do you believe that this story is realistic? Exaggerated? Common in real life? Rare?

7. Have you had any similar experiences?

8. In your opinion, should teachers use physical punishment? Should parents use it? Explain and be specific.

9. _____

This story is a folk tale about an old woman and her adult children.

The Wooden Chest

Part 1

There was once an old woman who had lost her husband and lived all   1
alone. She had worked hard all her life, raising a family and taking
in extra work as a seamstress. Now, in her old age, bad luck left her
penniless. Old and bent, she was unable to take care of herself any longer.
Her hands trembled too much to thread a needle, and her vision was
blurred too much for her to make a straight stitch.

The old woman had two sons and two daughters, but they were all   2
grown and married now, and they were busy with their own lives. They had
only enough time to stop by to see their mother once a week.

Gradually, the old woman grew more and more feeble, and her children   3
came by to see her less and less. "They don't want to be around me at
all any more," she told herself, "because they're so busy with their own lives

and afraid I'll become a burden." She stayed up all night worrying about what would become of her, until at last she thought of a plan.

The next morning the old woman went to see her neighbor, a carpenter, and asked him to give her a large, old chest that he didn't need any longer. Then she went to see another neighbor, a locksmith, and asked him to give her an old lock. Finally, she went to see still another neighbor, a glass blower, and asked him for all the unusable, old, broken pieces of glass that he had. 4

The old woman took the chest home, filled it to the top with the broken glass, locked it up tight, and put it under her kitchen table. The next time her children came to visit, they sat at the table and bumped their feet against it. 5

"What's in this chest?" they asked, looking under the table. 6

"Oh, nothing," the old woman replied, "just some things I've been saving." 7

The four children pushed at it with their feet and noticed how heavy it was. They kicked it and heard a rattling noise inside. "It must be full of all the gold she's inherited and saved over the years," they whispered to one another. 8

So they talked it over and decided they needed to guard the treasure. They made a plan to take turns living with the old woman, so they could look after her, too. In this way, the old woman always had one of her children living with her and helping her. This went on for some time. 9

Before you continue reading, what do you think will happen next?

_____

Part 2

At last the old woman grew sick and died. Her children gave her a very nice funeral, for they knew that a great fortune sat under the kitchen table, and they could afford to spend some money on the old woman now. 1

When the service was over, the four children hunted through the house until they found the key. Eagerly, they unlocked the chest. And, of course, they found it full of broken glass. 2

"What a rotten trick!" yelled the oldest child. "What a cruel thing to do to your own children!" 3

"But what else could she have done, really?" asked the next child. "We must be honest with ourselves. If it wasn't for this chest, we would have neglected our dear mother until the end of her days." 4

"I'm so ashamed of myself," sobbed the next child.   5

"And so am I," moaned the last child. "We forced our own mother to   6
use a trick to get our help."

The oldest child pushed the chest over to make sure there was nothing 7
valuable hidden among the glass pieces after all. He poured the broken
pieces out until the chest was entirely empty.

Then the four children stared silently at the floor for a long time.   8

Discussion Questions

*Discuss the following questions in small groups. Your instructor may ask you
to write down your answers. For number seven, write your own question
for discussion.*

1. In the first part of the folk tale, what problem does the old woman have?
   Pretend that you are the old woman, and explain or defend your position.

2. In the first part of the folk tale, what problem do the old woman's
   children have? Pretend that you are one of the children, and explain or
   defend your position.

3. The old woman finds a clever solution to her problem. In real life, however,
   what solution would you recommend?

4. How does the oldest child react to the truth about the contents of the trunk?
   How do the rest of the children react?

5. What is the message of this folk tale?

6. Do you agree or disagree with the message? Explain and support your
   opinion.

7. _____

   _____

This story is a folk tale about a woman, her two sons, and her rich friend.

Cornelia's Jewels

The sun was shining brightly on a glorious morning in ancient Rome. 1
Two boys were standing in a beautiful garden. They were looking at their
mother and her friend, who were walking among the flowers and trees.

"Have you ever seen a more attractive lady than our mother's friend? " 2
asked the younger boy, holding his tall brother's hand. "She looks like a
queen."

"She's pretty, but she's not as elegant as our mother," answered 3
the older boy. "She has rich clothing and shiny hair, but her face is not
honest and kind. It's our mother who looks like a queen."

"You're right," said the other. "No woman in Rome can match our dear 4
mother for her beauty and queenliness."

Soon, Cornelia, their mother, came down the path to speak with them. 5
She was simply dressed in a plain white robe. Her arms and feet were bare,

as this was the custom in those days; and she wore no rings on her fingers or sparkling necklaces around her neck. The only crown she wore consisted of her soft brown hair. A sweet smile lit up her noble face as she looked into her sons' proud eyes.

"My sons," she said, "I have something to tell you." They bowed to her, as Roman children were taught to do, and said, "What is it, Mother?"   6

"I'd like for you to have dinner with us in the garden. Our friend is going to show us that wonderful chest of precious jewels that we have all heard so much about."   7

The brothers looked shyly at their mother's friend. How could it be possible for her to have more jewels than the ones she wore? On her hands she had six rings with huge jewels, and around her neck, there were at least five strings of gold with jewels.   8

When the simple meal was over, a servant brought the chest out from the house. The lady opened it. It was filled with strings of gold, shining and glistening; ropes of pearls, as white as milk and as smooth as satin; heaps of rubies, as red as glowing coals; sapphires, as blue as the sky that summer day; emeralds, as green as new summer grass; and diamonds, flashing and sparkling like rays of the sun.   9

The brothers looked at the jewels for a long time. "Oh," whispered the younger boy. "If only our dear mother could have such beautiful things!" The older boy stood silent.   10

Finally, the lady closed the chest, and the servant took it away.   11

"Is it true, Cornelia, that you don't have any jewels?" asked the mother's friend? "You have no gold, no rubies, no pearls, no sapphires, no emeralds, no diamonds? Is it true, as I have heard people whisper, that you are poor?"   12

"No, I am not poor," answered Cornelia. As she spoke she gently pulled her sons to her side. "Here are my treasures. They are worth much more than all your gold and jewels."   13

Discussion Questions

Discuss the following questions in small groups. Your instructor may ask you to write down your answers. For number seven, write your own question for discussion.

1. What makes Cornelia's friend attractive? Explain and support your answer.

2. What makes Cornelia attractive?

3. Which woman places great importance on material wealth? Explain and support your answer.

4. How does Cornelia respond when her friend asks her if she's poor?

5. What do Cornelia's sons learn from their mother that day?

6. Do you agree or disagree with the message of the folk tale? Explain and support your opinion.

7. _____

   _____

ASSIGNMENT 8

This story is a modern folk tale about two men with different ideas about success.

The City Man and the Fisherman

A successful businessman from the city visited a small village next to the 1
sea. One morning he decided to take a walk along the beach. His time was
very limited, though, because he had to make several important
business calls soon. He stepped quickly and nervously, as he thought about
all his business obligations.

After a short time, the city man came across a fisherman sitting on the 2
sand. The fisherman was watching his small boat bobbing up and down in
the water and the birds circling lazily in the sky above. The city man
stopped and began a conversation with the fisherman.

"Good morning," he said, as he approached the fisherman who was 3
still sitting on the sand and enjoying the beautiful scenery.

The fisherman nodded a return greeting. 4

"Excuse me," continued the city man. "Why are you sitting on the sand? 5
Why aren't you out fishing?"

"I caught all the fish I need for today," replied the fisherman. 6

"Oh, but let me give you some good advice," the city man told the 7
fisherman. "If you fish for more than your usual amount, you will make more
money."

"Why should I make more money?" yawned the fisherman. 8

"Well, you would be able to buy more things, such as a bigger boat," 9
smiled the city man. He patted his expensive clothing as he spoke and
nodded toward the fisherman's small boat.

"Why do I need a bigger boat?" questioned the puzzled fisherman. 10

"Obviously," said the city man, "if you have a bigger boat, then you 11
can catch even more fish, and you can even hire a crew to work for you.
You can be the boss and wear expensive clothing."

"Why should I do that?" frowned the fisherman. "Then I'd have 12
to work twice as hard as I work now. Maybe three times as hard. Besides
expensive clothing is certainly no more comfortable than what I wear now."
He looked down at his simple, but comfortable clothing.

"Oh, you foolish man!" laughed the city man. "If you followed my 13
advice, then you would earn so much money that when you were ready to
retire, you could do anything with your time you wanted to do!"

The fisherman looked back up at the birds contentedly flying around in   14
wide circles and diving into the water for an occasional fish.

"But that's what I'm already doing," he smiled without looking back at   15
the city man.

Discussion Questions

Discuss the following questions in small groups. Your instructor may ask you to write down your answers. For number seven, write your own question for discussion.

1. What advice does the city man give to the fisherman?
2. How does the fisherman respond to the city man's advice?
3. Why does the city man believe that it is important to work?
4. Why does the fisherman reject the city man's advice?
5. What is the message of this modern folk tale?
6. In your opinion, which man's point of view is wiser? Explain and support your opinion.
7. _____

   _____

ASSIGNMENT 9

Select and read an excerpt from a short story or folk tale.

SECTION THREE

SUPPLEMENTARY MATERIAL FOR REFINING SKILLS

Distinguishing General and Specific ideas

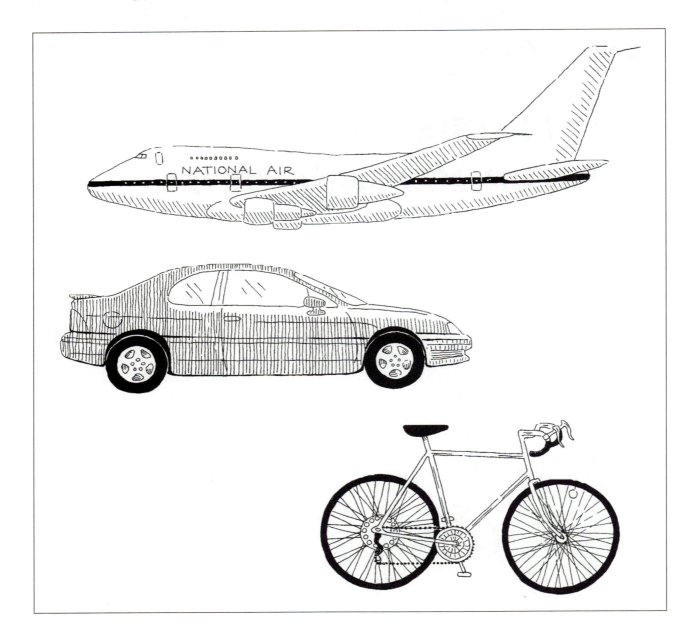

In order to organize your ideas effectively in a composition, you need to know which ideas are general and which ideas are specific. In Part 1, you will practice identifying general and specific ideas.

1. In the following list the more general idea "transportation" is circled. The other words are specific examples of different kinds of transportation.

train　　car　　(transportation)　　airplane　　bus　　bicycle

transportation　　　　　　→　　　　　　**GENERAL**

train, car, airplane,
bus, bicycle　　　　　　→　　　　　　**SPECIFIC**

2. In this list, the phrase that expresses a more general idea is circled. "A wonderful flight on Arabesque Airlines" expresses the main idea while the remaining four phrases give specific supporting details.

A. A wide selection of in-flight entertainment

B. Rapid check-in and baggage claim

(C.) A wonderful flight on Arabesque Airlines

D. Friendly flight attendants

E. Excellent food and service

A wonderful flight on Arabesque Airlines　　}　　**GENERAL**
Main Idea

A wide selection of in-flight entertainment
Rapid check-in and baggage claim　　　　　　}　　**SPECIFIC**
Friendly flight attendants　　　　　　　　　　　Support
Excellent food and service

 **PRACTICE A**

Each list contains one general idea (main idea) and several specific, supporting details. Circle the general idea in each list.

Example

carrots
string beans
corn
(vegetables)
peas

1. bananas
   peaches
   fruit
   watermelons
   apples

2. cars
   trucks
   motorcycles
   vans
   vehicles

3. Honda
   Ford
   makes of cars
   Mercedes
   Pontiac

4. entertainment
   going to movies
   bowling
   reading
   watching television

5. decent salary
   job benefits
   health insurance
   flexible hours
   discount on
      company merchandise

6. marriage
   children
   good job
   goals
   college degree

7. crime
   smog
   crowds
   disadvantages of cities
   the high cost of living

8. fresh air
   advantages of camping
   beautiful scenery
   away from crowds
   cheap

 **PRACTICE B**

The following lists consist of specific supporting details. For each list, write a general idea (main idea).

Examples

A. *subjects in science*
   chemistry
   biology
   anatomy
   geology

B. *reasons for disliking a job*
   low pay
   no medical benefits
   hard physical labor
   unfriendly coworkers

1. _____
   pork
   beef
   chicken
   lamb

2. _____
   a T-bone steak
   pork chops
   prime rib
   lamb chops

3. _____
   doughnuts
   potato chips
   candy
   french fries

4. _____
   ants
   termites
   flies
   cockroaches

5. _____

    cockroaches

    rats

    ants

    spiders

6. _____

    lung cancer

    emphysema

    bronchitis

    heart disease

7. _____

    reading action stories

    playing soccer

    going to movies

    drawing cartoons

8. _____

    reasonable pay

    friendly coworkers

    flexible hours

    located close to home

9. _____

    warm weather

    job opportunities

    plenty of fun things to do

    friendly people

10. _____

    to gain useful knowledge

    to please my parents

    to get a better job

    to meet interesting people

PRACTICE C

For each general idea (main idea), write three specific supporting details. Make your lists true for you. Then, working in small groups, compare your answers with your classmates.

Examples

A. My goals for the future

    finish law school

    become a successful lawyer

    find a suitable marriage partner

B. My reasons for learning English

    make my parents happy

    get a job in the computer industry in Toronto

    become a Canadian citizen

1. My hobbies or pastimes

    _____

    _____

    _____

    _____

2. My goals for the future

_____

_____

_____

_____

3. Problems in adjusting to a new culture

_____

_____

_____

_____

4. Things I miss (or do not miss at all) about a place where I used to live

_____

_____

_____

_____

5. Problems or benefits of living in large cities. (Choose one.)

_____

_____

_____

_____

6. What I like (or do not like) about living in this city, town, or area

_____

_____

_____

_____

7. Things in everyday life that bother me or delight me

_____

_____

_____

_____

8. The qualities of a good instructor

_____

_____

_____

_____

9. The qualities that I want in a boss, a friend, a neighbor, a husband/wife/
partner (Choose one person.)

_____

_____

_____

_____

10. The characteristics of my ideal job

_____

_____

_____

_____

PRACTICE D

Why is the following cartoon funny? Discuss your answer with your classmates.

"Crock" by Bill Rechin and Don Wilder. From the Los Angeles Times (June 25, 1993). Reprinted
with special permission of North American Syndicate.

Narrowing a Topic

Sometimes the topic your instructor gives you might be too general to write about in a short composition. Your task, then, is to narrow down this *general topic* to a more *specific topic*. Narrowing a topic is essential for effective and interesting writing.

For example, if you are asked to write on the general topic of "hobbies," you obviously cannot include all the different kinds of hobbies you know about in one short composition. Thus, you must select and write about one specific aspect of this topic.

For the general topic of "hobbies," here are some possible ideas for specific topics:

- Why Knitting Is a Great Hobby
- The Benefits of My Favorite Hobby: Soccer
- How I Got Started in Flower Arranging

 **PRACTICE**

Think about each of these general topics. Then, write a specific topic for each. Follow the example.

1. Fitness   Cycling is an enjoyable way to stay in shape.

2. Education

3. Being a parent

4. The future

5. Marriage

6. Health

7. Computers   _____

_____

8. Culture shock   _____

_____

9. Student life   _____

_____

10. Sports   _____

_____

11. Vacations   _____

_____

12. Politics   _____

_____

13. Current events   _____

_____

14. Science   _____

_____

Writing Titles

The title introduces your composition. It should be interesting enough to get the reader's attention before he or she starts reading.

Even though the title is the first part of your composition, this does not mean that you must come up with it before you start writing your first draft. In fact, many writers think of a title last. The advantage of adding the title later is that you will probably think of a more appropriate title.

PHYSICAL PRESENTATION OF TITLES

Read the following titles. Then, in pairs or in small groups, discuss and answer the questions that follow.

My Courageous Classmate Seynab

The Fugitive

A Minor Panic

Welcome to the Big City

A Misunderstanding

Freedom

Paris: My Dream Come True

A Truly Outstanding Teacher

An Exciting Trip across the Desert

Praying at a Japanese Shrine

My Lazy Cousin Fred

A Wise Saying from My Country: "A Friend in Need Is a Friend Indeed"

A Worthwhile Lesson in "A Rupee Earned"

Quitting an Unhealthy Habit: Smoking

What I Used to Be Afraid Of

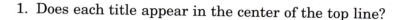

Discussion Questions

1. Does each title appear in the center of the top line?

2. Do the first and last words in the title start with a capital letter?

3. Are all words capitalized?

4. What kinds of words are NOT capitalized?

5. Does a capital letter appear after a colon (:)?

6. If a quotation appears in a title, is the first word inside the quotation capitalized?

7. Does a period appear at the end of a title?

GUIDELINES FOR WRITING TITLES

1. Center the title on the top line of the paper.

2. Capitalize the first and last words.

3. Capitalize the important words (the words with the most meaning).

4. Do not capitalize the following words unless they are the first or last words in the title, or they follow a colon (:)
   Articles: *a(n), the*
   Coordinators such as: *and, but, or*
   Prepositions such as: *in, on, at, for, with, from*

5. Use a capital after a colon (:).

6. If a quotation appears in a title, capitalize the first word of the quotation.

7. Do not use a period at the end, but you may use a question mark (?) or an exclamation mark (!).

PRACTICE A

Edit these titles. Use correct punctuation and capitalization.

1.

      M   B   M   E

my biggest mistake ever

2. Hope for the Future.

3. *A Terrifying Midnight Boat Ride*

4. I had a disappointing welcome in Chicago.

5. My Dreams For The Future

6. A True Saying: "a stitch in time is worth nine"

7. A summary and response to "risks"

8. **Never Again Disney World**

PRACTICE B

Read these compositions, and then think of an appropriate title for each.

Composition 1

_____

When I was in elementary school, my dream was to have an American-style bed. I asked my parents for such a bed, and to my delight, they bought me one for my birthday. The bed was a black bunk bed, with two levels. I slept on the lower level and used the upper level for playing. I kept all my toys on the upper level. I pretended that my bed was my castle. I was the king, and all my toys were my subjects who had to obey my commands. If they did not, they had to sleep under the bed in the dungeon. I felt very important. Even after I outgrew my bed, I enjoyed my memories of being the king of my castle.

Adapted from a composition by Muneyoshi Nishigaki

Composition 2

_____

When I remember the moonlit nights in Vietnam from twenty years ago,   1
I am filled with wonderful memories of the pleasures of the countryside. I
used to enjoy sitting in a chair in my garden on warm evenings
and watching how the moon lit up nature and turned it into a beautiful oil
painting. On the horizon, the river turned into a silvery finger in the upper
corner of the canvas. In the middle, points of light would dot the leaves of
the trees. In my own garden at the bottom of this painting, tiny pools of
water reflected the face of the moon.

To accompany this visual beauty, nature played a romantic song to me   2
in the form of the humming of the insects and the crackling of the wind in
the bushes. The breeze brought to my nostrils the smell of ripening rice from
the field behind my house. Sometimes, my tongue could even taste salt on
my lips, salt brought from the sea by the gentle wind. Often, when the fog
slowly rolled in, nature's canvas turned marvelously pale and dreamy, and
the moon turned into a soft glow. Then the wind would chill me just a little
and nudge me back into the warmth of my cozy house. Now, in my new
country, whenever I see a full moon, I am transported back to Vietnam, if
only in my dreams.

Adapted from a composition by Hoa Pham

Composition 3

_____

Mother love is one of the finest gifts I received as a child. I still remember
clearly when I was six years old and had the measles. I had to be isolated from
the rest of the family. I was sad about being alone, away from my brothers and
sisters, but Mom patiently explained why it had to be that way. She not only
took care of all my physical needs for the next two weeks, but she also cheered
me up and read to me for long hours. She even slept in my room on the floor,
and when I woke up, she stayed awake to comfort me. I hope I can be as good
a mother to my own children some day.

Adapted from a composition by Claudia Ortiz

4

Focusing on Main Ideas

The Main Idea

The first sentence of a short composition usually states the main idea and gives direction to the rest of the composition. The support, the body of your composition, provides specific details that explain and develop the main idea.

Students who are learning to write should state the main idea first. This makes it easier for the reader to understand and follow the ideas.

Example

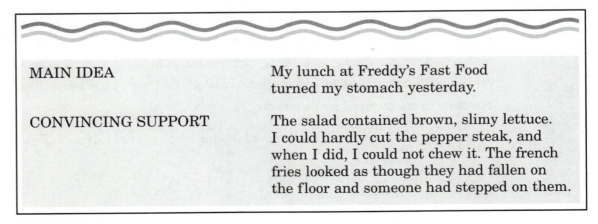

MAIN IDEA	My lunch at Freddy's Fast Food turned my stomach yesterday.
CONVINCING SUPPORT	The salad contained brown, slimy lettuce. I could hardly cut the pepper steak, and when I did, I could not chew it. The french fries looked as though they had fallen on the floor and someone had stepped on them.

Read these sentences. Circle the letter of the main idea in each group.

Example

   A. One thing I like to do is work in my garden.

  (B.) I enjoy several activities on my days off.

   C. Another activity I enjoy is going to movies.

   D. My favorite activity is going on picnics with my family.

1. A. I hate camping.

    B. The bugs bother me.

    C. Cooking over a campfire is unpleasant.

    D. I don't like sharing bathrooms with other campers.

2. A. It is close to the border, so I can visit Mexico often.

    B. San Diego is a great place to live.

    C. The weather is pleasant.

    D. It has plenty of interesting places to visit with the family.

3. A. Mouth, throat, or lung cancer rates are higher in smokers than in nonsmokers.

    B. Heart disease is more common in smokers than in nonsmokers.

    C. Emphysema strikes smokers more than nonsmokers.

    D. Smokers expose themselves to a variety of health problems.

4. A. I miss my mother's warm words of advice.

    B. I feel nostalgic when I think about the fun I used to have with my friends.

    C. I really miss my native country Syria.

    D. What makes me the saddest is being away from my family at holiday time.

5. A. The servers are friendly.

    B. The food is delicious.

    C. The atmosphere is pleasant.

    D. The Velvet Noodle is a great place to eat.

6. A. Spanish is a relatively easy language for an English-speaker to learn.

    B. The sounds of the letters are always the same.

    C. Many Spanish vocabulary words are similar to English words.

    D. It is easy to find people with whom one can practice Spanish.

7. A. They keep themselves clean.

   B. They have an independent personality.

   C. Cats make ideal pets.

   D. They can be affectionate.

8. A. My suitcase did not arrive at the airport with me.

   B. I had a terrible flight on Avio-Rapido last summer.

   C. The food was disgusting.

   D. The sound for the in-flight movie had a lot of static.

9. A. I dislike standing in long lines.

   B. I hate rush-hour traffic.

   C. The constant noise bothers me.

   D. I have several complaints about living in crowded cities.

10. A. I like the security of knowing that it is mine for as long as I want.

    B. I like owning my own home.

    C. I have the freedom to change anything I want in the house.

    D. Economically, I expect to come out ahead in the future.

Topics and Comments

A main idea contains two key elements. It usually states the topic and gives the writer's comment on that topic.

Topic:	The subject the writer is presenting
Comment:	The writer's intent for the topic: for example, personal feeling, opinion, belief, or other intent that will be developed with specific support

Example 1

Topic:	Common North American gestures
Comment:	Three often cause embarrassment to foreign students. (*writer's belief*)

Three common North American gestures often cause embarrassment to foreign students.

Example 2

Topic:	I, in Puerto Rico five years ago
Comment:	a fantastic vacation (*writer's personal feeling*)

I had a fantastic vacation in Puerto Rico five years ago.

PRACTICE A

Read the sentences that contain the main idea in the Practice on pages 185-186. In each sentence, underline the topic and circle the comment.

Example

(I enjoy several) activities on my days off.

PRACTICE B

For each of these main ideas, underline the topic and circle the comment.

1. I had a wonderful time on my vacation in Cancun last summer.

2. Smoking is dangerous for several reasons.

3. Walking is one of the best exercises known to humankind.

4. Small cars offer several advantages.

5. I have three favorite pastimes on weekends.

6. Ms. Jenkins, my writing instructor last semester, was a great teacher.

7. Owning your own home is not as enjoyable as many people think it is.

8. Living in a big city offers many advantages.

9. When a person gets married, he or she needs to be ready to accept certain responsibilities.

10. It is not easy to be a good parent.

11. When I lived in Colombia in the 1960s, I had a wonderful neighbor whose name was Amparo Hernández.

12. My geography professor at California State University at Long Beach was one of the worst instructors I have ever had.

Write a main idea for each of the following paragraphs.

Paragraph 1

_____

First of all, the pay is excellent. I make twice as much an hour as I did in my previous job. I also enjoy the people I work with. They are always friendly and helpful. Best of all, I have a good chance for advancement in the company. My boss told me the other day that he would like to give me a promotion within the year. I also enjoy having a company car. For all these reasons, I think I will stick with the company Acme Adhesives for a while.

Paragraph 2

_____

We had to wait for forty-five minutes before we got a table. During the entire time we waited, the headwaiter kept telling us it would be only five more minutes. Once we sat down, I noticed that my water glass had lipstick on it. The waiter replaced the glass with a clean one, but I got the feeling that he was annoyed with us for the rest of the evening. Even the food was disappointing. The vegetables were overcooked, the chicken was tough, and the rice was sticky. I will not listen to my boss's recommendation for a restaurant again.

Paragraph 3

_____

It offers a large variety of couches. The inventory includes styles you cannot find at most other stores. I found the salespeople patient and helpful. If you do not know exactly what you want, they will give you lots of information and let you take your time to make your choice carefully.

Most important, the prices are reasonable. The store guarantees the lowest prices in town. If you find the same couch somewhere else for less, the salespeople will refund the price difference. I really recommend the store Sofa So Good for anyone shopping for a new couch.

Paragraph 4

_____

_____

First of all, I enjoy playing with numbers. Even as a child I loved figuring out my math problems. It was like a fascinating game for me. Next, my father is an accountant. He has his own business, and he wants me to take over from him some day. Best of all, I got a scholarship for next year at USC in accounting. With this financial assistance, I can get my degree at a relatively low cost. With all these pluses, I would not even consider another major.

Paragraph 5

_____

_____

To begin with, the German shepherd next door barks a lot. When the owners are gone, the barking is nonstop. In addition to the constant dog barking, the teenage boy across the street loves heavy metal rock music. He plays it at full volume, especially when his parents are not home. He usually opens his front door and blasts the stuff until the roof shakes. Then, there is my neighbor in the house behind mine. She contributes her share of noise, too. Ms. Lyon yells at her kids constantly in a high-pitched screech. Her unpleasant screech echoes between the houses and carries right over to my bedroom. I wish I could move!

Practicing Support

The body, the middle and the longest part of your composition, provides support for the main idea. This support explains in a specific way what the main idea presents in a general way.

It's important for student writers to make sure that they include plenty of specific supporting details.

Note: In some cases, however, you may not need to provide details. For now, focus on providing plenty of specific supporting details. As you become more experienced, you will learn to recognize when not to provide details.

Specific Details

A common error in the support section of a composition is restating a general idea over and over by writing additional general statements. To avoid making this mistake, replace the general material with specific supporting details.

Compare the paragraphs on the opposite page. Notice that the second paragraph is more engaging and more interesting to read.

General

As one example of my recent bad luck, I was in an accident last month. I was not expecting it at all, so I was really shocked. It just happened. It was the other driver's fault, and I was completely surprised. I was not doing anything wrong. I could not believe I was in an accident. I never even saw it coming.

Specific

As one example of my recent bad luck, I was in a car accident last month. It happened during rush-hour on a rainy day, so I was driving especially carefully. I stopped at an intersection and I was changing the radio station when a Ford Mustang slammed into the back of my Honda Civic. I never even saw it coming.

Also, to provide interesting details, use specific words instead of general ones. For example, use "Ford Mustang" instead of "car" or "rose" instead of "flower." Compare these examples:

General	Specific
I *drove my car* on the *freeway.*	I *raced my Honda del Sol* on the *405 freeway.*
One child insulted the other.	*The six-year-old shouted to his playmate, "You're a jerk!"*
Pat *loved his teddy bear.*	Pat *took his teddy bear to bed with him every night.*

PRACTICE A

Rank the ideas in each list from the most general (1) to the most specific (4). Follow the example.

Example

_4_ a high-speed head-on collision

_2_ a car crash

_3_ a head-on crash

_1_ an accident

1. _____ a truck

   _____ a vehicle

   _____ a red Toyota pickup

   _____ a Toyota pickup

2. _____ a pippen apple

   _____ a green apple

   _____ a piece of fruit

   _____ a green piece of fruit

3. _____ a bird in a cage

   _____ an Amazon parrot in a wrought iron cage

   _____ a parrot in a cage

   _____ a pet

4. _____ a teenage girl with dark glasses

   _____ a female

   _____ an adolescent girl

   _____ a human being

5. _____ David teaches biology.

   _____ David teaches science.

   _____ David teaches Microbiology 4.

   _____ David teaches microbiology.

6. _____ Farida spends a lot of time in nature.

   _____ Farida backpacks into the High Sierras during school vacations.

   _____ Farida goes to the mountains whenever she can.

   _____ Farida camps in the mountains during school vacations.

7. _____ Ernst loves to paint.

   _____ Ernst loves art.

   _____ Ernst loves oil painting.

   _____ Ernst loves to paint portraits in oil.

The following exercise gives a main idea and pairs of supporting ideas. In each pair of supporting ideas, one pair is more specific than the other. Circle the letter of the idea that is more specific.

Fond Memories on a Starry Night

I really love the memories that I have of my mother, especially of the hot nights when we used to sleep in the backyard.

1. A. The sky was beautiful, and my mother and I spent many hours looking at it. It was really the most beautiful sky I have ever seen. My mother thought so, too.

    B. I remember that the blue sky had plenty of stars, and there was a full moon. The stars and moon shone with full brightness.

2. A. The view was gorgeous, and we saw many things in the sky. It was so beautiful.

    B. Sometimes we saw comets crossing the sky until they got lost in the distance.

3. A. My mother sat by my side, telling me stories about a princess, until I fell asleep.

    B. My mother told me stories until I fell asleep.

4. A. The next morning, the nice sounds from our neighborhood woke us up, but the most beautiful feeling was being with my mother.

    B. The next morning, the rooster's crowing waking me up was nice, but the most beautiful feeling was having my mother next to me.

Adapted from a composition by Gladys Monge

PRACTICE C

On a separate piece of paper, rewrite the following sentences, substituting the underlined general ideas for specific ones.

Example 1

The student made an excuse.

| The student | → | My classmate Sinan |
| made an excuse | → | said his son got sick, and he had to take his son to the doctor instead of writing his paper |

Example 2

An accident took place on the freeway.

| An accident took place | → | A car hit the center divider |
| on the freeway | → | on the 605 freeway |

1. He greeted her with a gift.

2. They bought a new car.

3. The car was dirty.

4. The cat relaxed.

5. The dog made us angry.

6. The children misbehaved.

7. I had car trouble.

8. The sales clerk (where?) was rude to me.

PRACTICE D

Imagine that you are writing a police report for one of the situations below. Write a paragraph explaining what happened. Include plenty of specific supporting details.

1. You were in a car accident.
2. You were the victim of a robbery.
3. You witnessed a crime.
4. A dog attacked your neighbor's child.

Relevant Support

Relevant support is directly related to the main idea. Every sentence in a composition needs to be relevant. If a sentence is irrelevant, you need to eliminate it.

In the following composition, the writer's comment is expressed through the word "enjoyable." There is, however, one sentence that is irrelevant because it does not support "enjoyable."

The Chinese New Year

The Chinese New Year is an enjoyable centuries-old spring festival. The fun lasts for several weeks. During this time, family and friends gather. People cook special foods, exchange gifts, and set off fire crackers. Sometimes people get hurt from the firecrackers. Often the community celebrates together with festivities such as the famous dragon parade. They wish each other *Gung Hay Fat Choy,* or Happy New Year! Without a doubt, this wonderful tradition will continue to delight people throughout the centuries.

Irrelevant sentence = Sometimes people get hurt from the firecrackers.

When you revise your composition, look for irrelevant material, and eliminate it.

 **PRACTICE A**

Read these compositions. One or more irrelevant sentences were added to each. Identify and cross out these irrelevant sentences. Be prepared to explain why you eliminated the sentences you identified as irrelevant.

Composition A

My Sweet Grandmother

The most important person in my childhood was my grandmother. I really loved going to her house during vacations. She would tell me fascinating stories about her life during World War II. She would also tell me fables, sometimes making up her own, with me as a beautiful, magic princess. Often we spent time in the forest picking raspberries and mushrooms. She taught me which ones to pick and which ones to avoid. Her next door neighbor got sick from mushroom poisoning one summer. When I was sad, my grandmother would rock me and sing to me. I can still hear her sweet and gentle voice. She died a few years ago, and I miss her very much.

Adapted from a composition by Teresa Poteranska

Composition B

My Castle

When I was in elementary school, my dream was to have an American-style bed. I asked my parents for such a bed, and to my delight, they bought me one for my birthday. I also wanted a guitar, but I did not get one. The bed was a black bunk bed with two levels. I slept on the lower level and used the upper level for playing. I kept all my toys on the upper level. I pretended that my bed was my castle. I was the king, and all my toys were my subjects who had to obey my commands. If they did not follow my commands, they had to sleep under the bed in the dungeon. I felt very important. My cousins did not like my game, though, so I did not like it when they came to visit. Even after I outgrew my bed, I enjoyed my memories of being the king of my castle.

Adapted from a composition by Muneyoshi Nishigaki

Composition C

My Favorite Hobbies

I enjoy three hobbies in my free time. My first hobby is playing with my two-year-old son. I especially like to teach him new words. He listens very carefully to me and copies what I say. I also like to take him for walks. When his small hands cling to my hand, I feel so close to him, and his wide smile warms my heart. If we play ball, he gets excited and screams with joy. Unfortunately, the ball makes the neighbor's dog bark, and this scares my son.   1

My second hobby is watching TV with my son. We watch Sesame Street together almost every day. It helps us learn English. The English on the news is too fast and really frustrates me. My son sits beside me, and sometimes we laugh until the tears come.   2

My third hobby is planting flowers in my garden. When I am watering the flowers, I feel a joy like the joy I feel when I am feeding my son. When I see the plants and flowers grow up inch by inch, I think of how my son is growing up, too. I wish the snails would stop eating my plants, though. These three hobbies fill me with a special pleasure like none I have ever experienced before.   3

Adapted from a composition by Lan-An Chang

 **PRACTICE B**

The ideas listed below are related to the general topic "owning a dog." The main ideas that follow, however, contain the same general topic but different comments. Under each main idea, write five relevant supporting details from the list. Some supporting details may apply to more than one main idea.

Feeding the dog every day, twice a day
Feeling safe and protected by the dog

Buying dog food

Having a constant friend

Putting up with dog odor

Repairing damage from the dog's chewing and digging

Killing fleas

Controlling the dog's barking at night

Paying veterinary bills when the dog gets sick

Buying equipment such as collars, leashes, dog beds,
brushes, flea shampoo

Bathing the dog

Getting up from bed to let the dog outside early
in the morning

Paying for a dog-sitter during vacations

Picking up dog dirt

Taking an eager companion for walks

Being warmly greeted when you return home

Spending money on annual shots

Paying for a dog license

Developing friendships with other dog owners

Main Idea A

Owning a dog costs too much money.

1. Buying dog food _____

2. _____

3. _____

4. _____

5. _____

Main Idea B

Owning a dog can be very satisfying.

1. _____

2. _____

3. _____

4. _____

5. _____

Main Idea C

Owning a dog is more trouble than it is worth.

1. _____

2. _____

3. _____

4. _____

5. _____

 **PRACTICE C**

Write a paragraph based on one of the main ideas given in Practice B. In your composition, support the main idea with plenty of specific supporting details. You are not limited to the information given. You can use your imagination.

Convincing Support

Read the following composition and then answer the questions that follow.

Risk

The main idea in Tim Timmons' paragraph "To Risk and Live Freely" is that we must take risks in life so that we do not regret what we have missed. I agree with what the author is saying. To give an example from my own life, I did not speak English when I moved to this country. At first, it did not matter to me. Later, though, when my son started speaking to me in English and I could not understand him, I felt unhappy. I began to think about enrolling in English classes. However, I was scared that I would feel ridiculous sitting in a classroom trying to make sounds that my mouth did not want to make. I also worried that people would make fun of me for going to school at my age. After struggling with my feelings for several weeks, I decided to take a risk and enroll in an English class. As I had thought, learning a new language was not easy, but I did not give up. At the end of the course, I felt proud of myself. Best of all, I was able to understand my son better when he spoke to me in English. Tim Timmons was absolutely right about risk, and I have no regrets.

Adapted from a composition by David Le

1. Why is David's composition convincing?

    _____

2. Have you had any similar experiences? Explain.

    _____

 **PRACTICE**

Read these six pairs of compositions. They are similar in topic. In your opinion, which composition in each pair is more convincing? Explain your reasons in the spaces provided. (Note: The student writer wrote the one that is more convincing in the opinion of the author of this text.)

1. Which composition is more convincing? _____

    Explain why. _____

    _____

    _____

Composition A

My Memory Box

One thing that I will never let go of is my collection of letters from my friends. I have gathered these letters for many years and kept them in my memory box. Whenever I feel blue or miss my old friends, I take my memory box out from deep inside my closet, handling it as if it were a treasure of jewels and gold. Then, I randomly choose one faded letter and read it. While my eyes move from word to word, I can see my friend's face, and I feel as though I am going back in time. Since I came to this country, my memory box has helped me remember how important my friends are to me. It is my most valuable possession, and I plan to keep on collecting letters for the rest of my life.

Composition B

My Memory Box

One thing that I will never let go of is my collection of letters from my friends. I have gathered these letters for many years and kept them in my memory box. The box is made of dark wood with colorful designs of hearts and flowers painted on the top. It is fairly large, with enough room to keep lots of letters. I keep them there in groups organized by my friends' names and the dates. Rubber bands keep the individual groups together so that they will not get mixed up. A few months ago when I was sick, I reread some of the letters from the box. They kept me entertained while I watched television. I plan to keep on collecting letters for the rest of my life.

Adapted from a composition by Amy Choi

2. Which composition is more convincing? _____

Explain why. _____

_____

_____

Composition A

My Father the Nature Lover

My father loved nature and made it his favorite hobby. He did not like to grow flowers in flowerpots. Instead, he believed that all plants should grow up in a natural environment, such as a forest or a meadow. Also, he used to take me out into the fields far away from home. We drove several hours out of the city where we hiked on trails for miles, sometimes all day; but we never got tired because we were having so much fun. Sometimes he helped me catch insects. We would study them for a while and then decide to let them go because there was so much more up ahead for us to look at. On our way home, we would stop at a small cafe for lunch. My dear father really loved nature, and I have learned to enjoy it too, thanks to him.

Composition B

My Father the Nature Lover

My father loved nature and made it his favorite hobby. He did not like to grow flowers in flowerpots because he thought plants needed to set their roots down in the ground and grow up turning their faces toward the sun. Also, he used to take me out into the fields far away from streets and cars and houses. We would hike for many happy hours in nature's yard, and sometimes he helped me catch insects such as dragonflies, beetles, and butterflies. After we looked at them up close to appreciate their beauty more, my father always let them go. He said, "I know you want to go home after sunset. All living creatures want this." My dear father taught me that we should love every living thing in the world.

Adapted from a composition by Kyoko Andoh

3. Which composition is more convincing? _____

   Explain why. _____

   _____

   _____

Composition A

My First Doll

When I was a child, my favorite possession was a special toy that my mother gave me. On my tenth birthday, she gave me a box, but she didn't tell me what was inside. All she said was, "I want you to have a big surprise." When I opened the box, my eyes opened wide with joy, as a beautiful doll looked back at me from the box. She wore a long dress, and her eyes moved when I moved her body. I loved her immediately. When I went to sleep, she slept beside me, and when I woke up, she woke up, too. I loved her like a sister, and told her all my secrets. She listened to all my thoughts, always with a smile of approval on her shiny face. She was my special friend, and I will always miss her.

Composition B

My First Doll

When I was a child, my favorite possession was a special toy that my mother gave me. On my tenth birthday, she gave me a box that was wrapped in blue and gold paper. In this beautiful box was a new doll. I was so happy to get her, especially since all my friends had new dolls, and I wanted one, too. When my neighbor friend came over with her doll, we played house together for hours at a time. My doll was almost the same as hers, but with different dresses. We changed our dolls' clothes, fed them with pretend food, and took them for walks. We pretended we were their mothers and scolded them when they misbehaved. My doll was very important to me, and I will always miss her.

Adapted from a composition by Thy Nguyen

4. Which composition is more convincing? _____

   Explain why. _____

   _____

   _____

Composition A

The Blue Blanket

I will always remember with much fondness the beautiful blue blanket my grandmother gave me when I was a tiny baby. Blankets are important to young children, and I was no exception. A small child can have a blanket for many years, and even if it gets old, dirty, and torn, the child will still love it. The child carries the blanket around all day, and when night comes, the blanket helps the child get to sleep. Nobody can convince the child that the blanket is old. I guess children need something familiar to comfort them, and the blanket becomes a habit. If someone tries to take the blanket away from the child, he or she puts up a big fuss and has a hard time sleeping without it. Nothing a parent does can convince the child that the blanket is too old and no good anymore. Maybe the blanket feels like a friend to the child, and maybe the child feels unsafe without it. When the child gets a new blanket, it takes a long time to get used to it. That is what happened to me. I finally got used to my new blanket, but I will never forget my old blue one.

Composition B

The Blue Blanket

I will always remember with much fondness the beautiful blue blanket my grandmother gave me when I was a tiny baby. My mother says that I held it tightly to my body, even when I was only six months old. By the time I was two, I had to have my blue blanket with me when I went to bed, or I could not sleep. It made me feel loved, safe, and protected. By the time I was five years old, my precious blanket was full of holes, and eventually, it tore into two pieces. One day, my mother threw it away and bought me a new one — a yellow one. That night, I could not sleep, and I cried for my blue blanket. My mother tried to convince me that the new yellow blanket was better. I screamed at her, "No! It's not the same!" I felt abandoned by a protective friend, and I cried myself to sleep every night for the next month. I finally got used to the yellow blanket, but I never loved it as much as I loved my old blue one.

Adapted from a composition by Chamroeun Thong

5. Which composition is more convincing? _____

   Explain why. _____
   _____
   _____

Composition A

The Beautiful Woodland

When I was a child, I would often visit a beautiful woodland near my house. As soon as I got there, I would lie down in the soft, fresh-smelling grass and look up at the natural world above me. Bushes surrounded my grassy bed, and tiny blue and yellow flowers grew in small bouquets. Above the bushes and flowers, tall, leafy trees and pines reached for the sky, and I enjoyed studying the shapes of the leaves outlined against the sky. I especially liked when the wind blew gently on the leaves and they would fall. They were like parachutes landing on the soft ground. When I closed my eyes, I could hear the birds singing and the rabbits moving through the dry leaves. All of these noises sounded to me like nature's orchestra in the middle of the peaceful forest.

Often I would choose one flower with a sweet fragrance and take it home with me along with some small pieces of pine. Then I would press the flower and pine pieces in a book. I loved their sharp, sweet smell. Later, when I was at school, I would inhale their perfume and recapture the peacefulness of the beautiful woodland.

As an adult, I still enjoy visiting quiet places in the forest. Now, though, my pleasure is doubled, because I have a daughter to take with me to share this joy.

Composition B

The Beautiful Woodland

When I was a child, I would often visit a beautiful woodland near my house. As soon as I got there, I would lie down in the fresh-smelling grass and look up at the natural world above me. There were a lot of plants around me, and many beautiful flowers grew nearby. In addition to the plants and flowers, I could see lots of trees. They were so big and beautiful. It was especially enjoyable when the wind blew, and it blew often in this place. Even though wind can be a bother at times, sometimes it adds to the pleasure of a short stay in nature. Another pleasure in nature is the sounds that a person can hear there, such as birds singing and other sounds. When there are enough different sounds, I feel as though I am attending a special concert by nature in the middle of the peaceful forest.

I used to like to press flowers from this beautiful place in books. I would pick lots of flowers and press them in school books. Sometimes, when I opened one of the books with the pressed flowers, the flowers would fall out and surprise me. Once in a while, they even fell on to the floor and broke apart, and I'd have to pick them up and put them back into the book. If I was at school, I'd worry that my teacher would get angry with me for not paying attention to the lesson.

2

As an adult, I still enjoy visiting quiet places in nature. Now, though, my pleasure is doubled, because I have a daughter to take with me to share this joy.

3

Adapted from a composition by Maria Acero

6. Which composition is more convincing? _____

Explain why. _____

_____

_____

Composition A

The Rice Field Ghost

The most frightening experience I've ever had happened when I was seven years old. My sister and I went to a movie one evening. After the movie, we stopped with friends for a snack at a small restaurant, where we stayed until it started to get dark. Our friends had to get home, so we decided it was time for us to go home, too.

1

On the way home, we decided to take a shortcut across a rice field. Nothing was nearby, only a few tombs here and there. We were alone and didn't have much light. Half way across, a strong and sudden wind came up and made terrible noises. I've never heard such terrible noises. We were really scared. To add to this, we heard another sound that frightened us. It didn't sound human, and it didn't sound like any animal we had ever heard. Our fear made us walk faster, and at that point our light went out.

2

Looking ahead, we saw a scary figure ahead of us. It looked like a ghost, and it crossed the path ahead of us. We were really scared. We ran the other way, but had a lot of trouble running in the dark. All we could do was scream and try to get away. Luckily, our screams were heard, and we were rescued. 3

I don't know if what we saw was real or not, but since that night, I've never walked in places like that in the darkness again. 4

Composition B

The Rice Field Ghost

The most frightening experience I've ever had happened when I was seven years old. My sister and I were on the way home from a movie, when we decided to take a shortcut across a rice field. There were no houses nearby, only a few tombs here and there. My sister walked in front of me with a torch in her hand. Half way across, a strong and sudden wind came up and made the trees sound as though they were cracking. This alone was scary enough, but to add to this, we heard thumping and then an inhuman-sounding cry. Our fear made us walk faster, and at that point the wind blew out our torch. 1

Looking ahead, we saw a lady in a white dress and long, flowing hair covering her face, flying across our path in slow motion. Terrified, we ran in the other direction through the night, tripping a few times over obstacles hidden in darkness. The faster we ran, the closer the lady in white seemed to follow us. All we could do was scream and try to get away. Luckily, our two brothers heard our screams and rushed to our rescue. 2

I don't know if we saw a real ghost or not, but since that night, I've never walked near tombs in the darkness again. 3

Adapted from a composition by Zena Hai

Read the following composition. Based on what you know about support, discuss what makes Bob's description of his childhood home in the winter so successful. Use the space provided.

Warmth in the Winter

I felt an especially close personal bond to my family's warm house in   1
the snowy wintertime during school vacations. It was located at the edge of
a hilly forest near a big lake in the heart of Europe. After I had skated for

a full day with my junior hockey team, the evening fell very fast. Shadows began to veil the lake, and the air suddenly became as cold as the ice we skated on. The warmth of home called to me, just a walk away through the snowy fields.

When I opened the front door to my house, the aroma from my mother's cooking immediately surrounded me. I entered into a comfortable, square living room, well protected from the cold, windy weather outside. A soft light glowed in the corner. My initial step into this loving interior gave me a magical feeling. After I changed into thick, warm socks and slippers, I sat down to a large bowl of spicy, hot soup that my dear mother had prepared for my return. After I ate, I would join my father on the couch, where he often read a book to me, discussed my hockey games, and exchanged jokes with me. My father's calm, deep voice and the warmth of his love filled my tired body.

I did not realize then how lucky I was. In later years, though, I came to understand how safe and peaceful my childhood had been in that warm and cozy house in Czechoslovakia.

Adapted from a composition by Bob Krupka

_____

_____

_____

_____

One of the reasons that Bob's composition is so successful is that his details create an experience that comes alive for us. These details appeal to our senses.

Read Bob's composition again. This time underline the words that appeal to our senses. (The five senses are sight, sound, touch, taste, and smell.) Write the corresponding senses in the margin.

 **PRACTICE A**

In pairs or small groups, discuss why the student composition on the next page is so effective. Write your comments in the space provided.

Moonlit Nights

When I remember the moonlit nights in Vietnam from twenty years ago, I am filled with wonderful memories of the pleasures of the countryside. I used to enjoy sitting in a chair in my garden on warm evenings and watching how the moon lit up nature and turned it into a beautiful oil painting. On the horizon, the river turned into a silvery finger in the upper corner of the canvas. In the middle, points of light would dot the leaves of the trees. In my own garden at the bottom of this painting, tiny pools of water reflected the face of the moon.

1

To accompany this visual beauty, nature played a romantic song to me in the form of the humming of the insects and the crackling of the wind in the bushes. The breeze brought to my nostrils the smell of ripening rice from the field behind my house. Sometimes, my tongue could even taste salt on my lips, salt brought from the sea by the gentle wind.

2

Often, when the fog slowly rolled in, nature's canvas turned marvelously pale and dreamy, and the moon turned into a soft glow. Then the wind would chill me just a little and nudge me back into the warmth of my cozy house. Now, in my new country, whenever I see a full moon, I am transported back to Vietnam, if only in my dreams.

3

Adapted from a composition by Hoa Pham

_____

_____

_____

_____

PRACTICE B

On a separate piece of paper, write a description of one of the following topics. Include words that appeal to at least four of the five senses: sight, sound, touch, taste, and smell.

1. A restaurant you like

2. The place where you live

3. A beautiful place in nature

4. A vacation spot at the beach

5. A public place in your hometown, such as a park or a marketplace

6. A farm

7. The school cafeteria

8. A movie theater

9. A church, synagogue, temple, shrine, or other place of worship

10. A hospital

11. A place from your past that holds a special place in your heart

Your ideas for a topic

12. _____

13. _____

14. _____

15. _____

Practicing Conclusions

The concluding sentence, usually the last, ties together your entire composition. A concluding sentence can offer a summary of the main points discussed in the paragraph; it can offer a solution or prediction. The writer can also make a recommendation concerning the ideas presented in the paragraph. Without a conclusion, however, the reader wonders "And so . . . ?"

Read the following sample composition from "Getting Started." It has no conclusion.

My Job Dissatisfaction

Lately, I have been unhappy with my job as a cashier at McBuns. First, the hours are a hardship for me. I work from three to eleven in the evening, and I have trouble getting up the next morning for my math class. Next, the pay is miserable. I am making only twenty cents above minimum wage. Last, the people I work with are unfriendly. They never smile or want to be sociable.

Study the following common conclusion types and the examples that would be appropriate for "My Job Dissatisfaction."

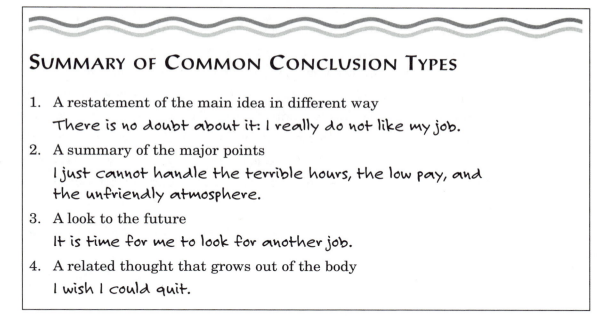

SUMMARY OF COMMON CONCLUSION TYPES

1. A restatement of the main idea in different way

   There is no doubt about it: I really do not like my job.

2. A summary of the major points

   I just cannot handle the terrible hours, the low pay, and the unfriendly atmosphere.

3. A look to the future

   It is time for me to look for another job.

4. A related thought that grows out of the body

   I wish I could quit.

Often, the third and fourth types of conclusions are stronger than the first two types. Many conclusions combine more than one technique.

 **PRACTICE**

The following compositions have no conclusions. Write your own appropriate conclusion for each.

Composition A

The Finest Gift of Love

Mother love is one of the finest gifts I received as a child. I still remember clearly when I was six years old and had the measles. I had to be isolated from the rest of the family. I was sad about being alone away from my brothers and sisters, but Mom patiently explained why it had to be that way. She not only took care of all my physical needs for the next two weeks, but she also cheered me up and read to me for long hours. She even slept in my room on the floor, and when I woke up, she stayed awake to comfort me.

Adapted from a composition by Claudia Ortiz

Your conclusion: _____

_____

_____

Composition B

Money and Happiness

Having money does not guarantee happiness. My family was not rich, but we were happy for many years. Then one day, unexpectedly, my mother inherited my grandmother's fortune, and soon we were arguing about what to do with our riches. We fought over the jewelry, until our unhappiness tore the family apart. I wanted us to be the way we were before we got so rich with material things. Luck changed for us, though, when we came to this country. We lost everything on the way. However, step by step, we got back what we had lost and needed most: our love for each other.

Adapted from a composition by Ngi Nguyen

Your conclusion: _____

_____

_____

Composition C

Honesty Is the Best Policy

"Honesty is the best policy." This famous saying from Miguel de Cervantes' *Don Quixote* means that we have to be honest in all situations. I agree, especially because of what happened to my grandfather about three years ago. He got sick, and his doctor diagnosed him with cancer. His doctor put him in the hospital, but he did not tell my grandfather the truth right away. During the first three months in the hospital, my grandfather's energy level dropped constantly, and the cancer just kept getting worse. Then the doctor told him the truth — that he had terminal cancer and would live for only a few months. I thought my grandfather would not be able to handle the truth, but a strange thing happened. He began enjoying his life. He even developed enough energy to leave the hospital occasionally to do whatever he really wanted to do. To my surprise, my grandfather lived for another year.

Adapted from a composition by Tomo Wakamatsu

Your conclusion: _____

_____

_____

Composition D

Classroom Procedures in Taiwan

In Taiwan, instructors and students follow several classroom procedures. First, students have to show their respect to instructors. This is because of the influence of Confucian philosophy, which dates back several thousand years. Therefore, when the instructor enters the room, the class leader says loudly, "Stand up," and then the students stand up, bow, and say, "Good morning, Teacher!" Second, students follow strict rules during the class. They have to raise their hands and call the instructor "teacher," if they have any questions. Also, if they fail to pay attention one hundred percent, the instructor punishes them. Third, the instructor does most of the talking. Most of the time, the instructor explains the contents of the textbook. Sometimes he asks students to answer questions or practice a problem in front of the class.

Adapted from a composition by Chengkuo Shin

Your conclusion: _____

_____

_____

Composition E

Culture Shock

I started experiencing culture shock shortly after I arrived in this country. In Vietnam, when young people speak to an elder, they have to be very respectful. They have to use different ways of addressing people based on age. If a young person makes a bad guess and refers to an older person with the wrong term, the older person will get upset. However, English does not have different ways to address people, and this made me crazy when I was a new arrival in this country. I felt uncomfortable when I talked with my teacher, for example, because the word "you" sounded so disrespectful. Instead of using the word "you," I began to say "Teacher! Teacher!" When my friends laughed at me, I started using the word "you" to teachers, even though I felt and still feel impolite and guilty when I say "you."

Adapted from a composition by Huyen Tran

Your conclusion: _____

_____

_____

Composition F

Wasters of My Time

Two things waste a lot of my time. The first one is preparing and   1
eating food. Every morning it takes me about a half hour to make my
breakfast and my lunch. I am not even counting the time it takes to eat!
When I come home at night, I have to prepare dinner for my family. It takes
over two hours to cook, eat, and clean up. The total is about three hours a
day! Then, when there is a special occasion, a birthday, a visit, or a
holiday, I spend an entire morning or afternoon cooking. I am really fed up
with it! Sometimes I wish there were some magic machines to make us not
be hungry so that we do not have to eat and waste so much time.

The second time waster for me is waiting for things, such as for the bus,   2
standing in line at the supermarket, or waiting for people to take care of their
responsibilities at work. Just waiting for the bus, for example, takes me an
hour a day; if I am late (because it takes so long to prepare food and eat in
the morning), I have to spend another hour waiting for the next bus. Waiting
for things just steals a lot of my time.

The total time I waste each day is over four hours. This is half of an eight-   3
hour work day!

Adapted from a composition by Thanh Le

Your conclusion: _____

_____

_____

Deciding on Paragraph Size

Short compositions often consist of one paragraph, especially in beginning and intermediate writing classes. If, however, a paragraph becomes long, you may need to break the material into several shorter paragraphs.

Look at this sample composition. It is fairly long and had to be broken into several shorter paragraphs.

First, read this narration, then answer the question that follows.

Climbing Mt. Fuji

When my husband and I climbed Mt. Fuji, the tallest mountain in Japan, five years ago, I experienced pure joy. It was a beautiful day at the beginning of the summer. Before we started climbing, we prayed at a shrine for our safety. Some people started climbing from the middle of the mountain (they got there by car), but we ventured to climb from the bottom. On our way up, several cars passed us, but we were enjoying the landscape of the river and hills. 1

When we arrived at the middle of the mountain, we had lunch there. As we ate, we looked around at the restful scene of trees, flowers, and other 2 plants. The fresh air refreshed our spirits. Then we started climbing again. Gradually, we had to breathe harder because of the altitude, and we saw more and more alpine plants. That night, we slept in a cottage for a few hours.

The next morning, we got up before dawn so that we could see the   3
sunrise, for good luck. While we climbed, the sky brightened, and we stopped for a few minutes to admire the gorgeous first light of day. This light threw an impressive glow on to the plants and rocks. At that point, I felt the glow of joy. It felt absolutely wonderful to be alive! After a while, we resumed climbing. We were breathing harder and harder, and we had to concentrate on climbing one step at a time.

Finally, when the top of the mountain was in sight, my footsteps became   4
very heavy, and my feet hurt. Then I looked ahead and saw my husband reach the top. This gave me strength to continue on after him. With renewed effort, I made it to the top, too! At that point, all my tiredness and the pain in my feet disappeared. I felt ecstatic, as if I were in heaven. I will always be very glad I had the chance to climb the tallest mountain in Japan, Mt. Fuji.

Adapted from a composition by Hideyo Masuya

How did the writer decide where to break the material into shorter paragraphs?

Your answer: _____

_____

_____

 **PRACTICE**

The following composition can be broken into several shorter paragraphs. Draw a check mark at the places where you would break this paragraph into shorter ones.

Moving Out of the Big City

There are several reasons why people move out of the big city every year. First, many people are unhappy with the air quality. For example, the smog continues to get worse in big cities every year, and some people develop allergies to the air pollution. Another reason people move is to escape the traffic and crowds. These days freeways are always congested. It could take hours to drive twenty miles across town. Also, the stores and malls are always so crowded that people have to wait in long lines to pay for their merchandise. Next, people in the inner city are getting tired of the high crime rate. Because drugs cause such a severe problem in the city, the rate of homicides continues to rise. The only solution for some people is to move to a safer environment. Finally, lots of people move out of the big city because they cannot find housing there at a reasonable cost. For example, young couples cannot afford to buy their own house. Also, retired people cannot live on a retirement pension with the high cost of living in big cities. Students, however, probably face the toughest hardships of all, because their income is usually lower than average, and they often have to live with a roommate or relative. It is unfortunate that many people have to leave the city that may have been their home for many years.

How did you decide to break the paragraph where you did?

_____

_____

_____

APPENDICES

The Product—Three Essentials

Obviously, process writing leads to a product: the finished composition that you turn in to your instructor. The following three essentials will guide you toward a successful piece of writing.

The First Essential: Clear, Convincing Content

Clear, convincing content consists of the following:

1. MAIN IDEA	The composition contains one clear main idea.
2. CONVINCING SUPPORT	The support develops the main idea with plenty of relevant, specific supporting details.
3. APPROPRIATE TONE	The composition expresses the appropriate level of formality, based on the audience and the guidelines the instructor presents in class. (Find out which writing style your instructor recommends. Some instructors may prefer a personal, subjective tone; however, others may prefer a more objective, formal tone. Also, the tone of your writing may vary, depending on the audience.)
	Many instructors encourage the development and expression of each student's individual voice. (Voice refers to your writing sounding like the real you.)

You are a unique person with a unique collection of life experiences and a unique voice.

Your writing voice can be compared to your talking voice on the telephone. Those who know you can recognize your voice immediately. This is due to your vocal quality, your choice of vocabulary, the way you form your sentences, and what you say. Your individual combination of these characteristics is unique.

Your speaking voice and your writing voice "sound" like you to those who know you.

When you write, don't be afraid to use your own unique voice. Few people want to read material that sounds like it was created by a computer. Be yourself. Be real. In this way, you will communicate authentically, and your audience will take greater interest in what you "say."

The Second Essential: Clear Organization

Clear organization consists of the following, in the order it appears below. (The author of this book recommends this order for developing writers.)

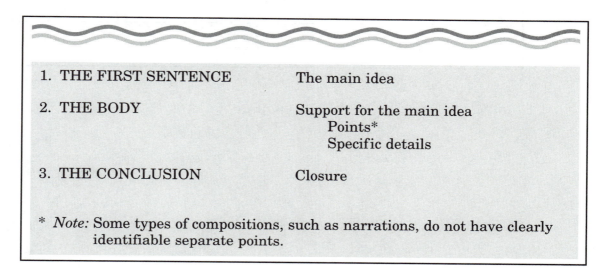

1. THE FIRST SENTENCE   The main idea

2. THE BODY   Support for the main idea
            Points*
            Specific details

3. THE CONCLUSION   Closure

* *Note:* Some types of compositions, such as narrations, do not have clearly identifiable separate points.

The Third Essential: Standard Grammar

A final draft that uses standard grammar and is relatively free from errors is an excellent goal for writers. Developing writers, however, need to put the emphasis on progress, not perfection.

Not all grammar points are equally important. The following is a list of some of the grammar points that your instructor may want you to focus on when you proofread and edit your composition.

Note: Your instructor may add or delete items from the list.

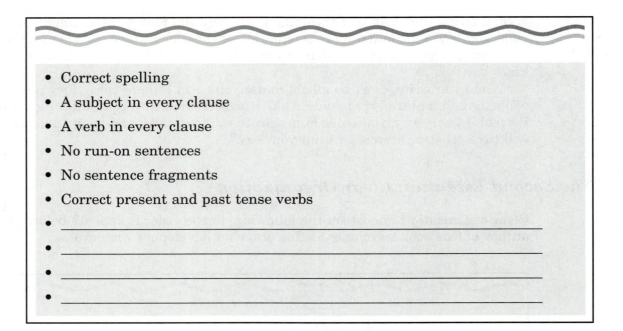

- Correct spelling
- A subject in every clause
- A verb in every clause
- No run-on sentences
- No sentence fragments
- Correct present and past tense verbs
- _____
- _____
- _____
- _____

APPENDIX **2**

Process Writing

Writing for college and professional purposes normally consists of a process with several steps and activities.

Step 1: *Preparing to Write*

The following activities will help you prepare to write.

DETERMINING YOUR AUDIENCE

Before you begin writing, you need to identify your audience. Knowing your audience helps you write appropriately for that specific person or group. Is your instructor the only person who will read your composition? Will other students in your class read it? Is the purpose of the assignment to help you practice writing for your other academic classes such as history, science, or business?

For example, if you are writing about an interview of one of your classmates, and your classmates will read your composition, your instructor might advise you to write in an informal style. In this case, your subjective, personal voice is appropriate. On the other hand, if you are writing about a scientific process — a paper you might write for a microbiology class, for example, then your instructor might advise you to write in an objective, formal style. If you have any doubts about your audience, check with your instructor.

WARMING UP: RESPONDING TO OTHERS' WRITING

Each chapter of this text opens with several sample compositions, most by student writers. An excellent way to warm up to writing your own composition is to write a response to one of the sample compositions. This warm-up usually contains three parts:

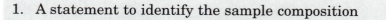

1. A statement to identify the sample composition
2. A summary of the most important ideas
3. A response: your ideas or opinions, based on the ideas in the composition

See the example in Chapter 2, page 36.

SELECTING A TOPIC

Your instructor will guide you in selecting a topic. If you have several to select from, choose the topic that interests you the most. Make sure that you can supply plenty of specific supporting details for your topic.

EXPLORING IDEAS

Listing Ideas. For this technique, you will make a list of ideas related to your topic. Allow your mind to explore, and write whatever comes to mind, without judging or censoring anything. You will find that one idea leads to another. In this way, you will discover useful ideas that you may have overlooked otherwise. Do not worry about correct grammar, spelling, or punctuation Do not try to write complete sentences. Instead, write key words, phrases, and ideas. See the examples in Chapter 1, page 11, and Chapter 4, page 78.

Interviewing. For some writing assignments, you may write about other people or about information you get from other people on a specific topic. Perhaps you will write a composition of introduction about one of your classmates, or perhaps you will report on the opinions of several classmates. In both cases, you will need to prepare and carry out an interview (or several interviews). See the assignment in Chapter 1.

Listing Interview Questions. Before you meet with your interview partner(s), decide what kind of information you want from the interview, and then write a list of questions to ask your partner(s).

Conducting an Interview. When you meet with your partner(s), refer to your list of prepared questions. You are not necessarily limited to these questions, however.

Let's assume for a moment that your assignment is to write a composition about another student in class. While you are interviewing your partner, the conversation will naturally lead you to additional questions. By all means, ask them! These additional questions often produce the most interesting information about your partner and will provide you with excellent material for your composition. Of course, you need to take notes during the interview. You will use these notes later when you write your composition. These notes do not have to be in complete sentences, and the grammar does not have to be perfect. The purpose of these notes is simply to provide you with the information you need in order to write your composition.

Brainstorming. Brainstorming consists of asking yourself questions about your topic. You can use the basic question words to help you get started:

Who . . . ?	What . . . ?
When . . . ?	How . . . ?
Where . . . ?	Why . . . ?

If your assignment is to write about an embarrassing situation, for example, you might ask yourself the following questions:

Who was involved in the situation?
When did it take place?
Where did it take place?

What happened?

How did you feel about it?

Why did you feel the way you did about it?

Take notes for the answers. See the example in Chapter 2, page 37.

Discussing Your Topic with Others. For this technique, you will discuss your topic with your classmates or others. Your instructor may ask you and your classmates to contribute ideas in a full class discussion. As an alternative, your instructor may ask you to meet in small groups to exchange ideas.

Through discussion, your classmates will give you ideas. In addition, your classmates' ideas will help you uncover ideas of your own.

Discussion doesn't have to end in the class. Often, you will find that if you continue discussing the topic with your family or friends outside of class, you will develop additional ideas.

If you do not have the opportunity to discuss ideas with your classmates, make sure you make time to do this outside of class with family or friends.

Freewriting. For this technique, you will write freely about your topic. As you did for the listing technique, allow your mind to explore, and write everything that comes to mind, without judging or censoring anything. You will find that one idea leads to another. In this way, you can discover useful ideas that you may have overlooked otherwise. When you freewrite, do not worry about correct grammar, spelling, or punctuation. If you get stuck, simply write "I'm thinking about (my topic), and the ideas are starting to come to me" over and over until the ideas start to come to you. See the example in Chapter 3, page 59.

Clustering. For this technique, you will start by writing your topic in the center of a sheet of paper and then drawing a circle around the topic.

Next, allow your mind to come up with ideas freely; accept any idea that is related to your topic in any way. Write these ideas in positions around the topic. Circle each new idea, and draw a line to connect it with the topic. Continue in the same manner with additional ideas.

Connect each new idea with the one before it. One idea will lead to another. In this way, you will end up with a page of ideas that branch out from your original topic.

After you have produced a full page of ideas, select one branch or several related branches to focus on in your composition. See the example in Chapter 6, page 118.

Reading. Your instructor may ask you to read an outside source such as an article, short story, or short novel. For some types of assignments, you can use the ideas in the reading to help point you toward your own ideas. For other types of assignments, your instructor may ask you to respond directly to the ideas in the reading. See the examples in Section Two — *Composing: Responding to Outside Sources.*

Step 2: Planning and Organizing

Before you write your first draft, you need to plan ahead and organize your ideas. Make sure you have (1) one main idea and (2) enough specific supporting details for your main idea. Also, select an order that is effective and easy for the reader to follow.

Some experienced writers can organize their ideas in their head. Others prefer organizing their ideas on paper. For you, as a developing writer, it may be very helpful to organize your ideas on paper.

NUMBERING IDEAS

This technique is especially effective after you have produced a list of ideas in Step 1.

- Look at your list of ideas, and identify a main idea. Write *M* in front of the main idea.
- Often, you might not find the exact words you need for a main idea. In this case, write a main idea and add it to your list.
- After you have a main idea, identify and number the ideas that support your main idea. Each number represents one point and the details that support it.
- You can add ideas to your list at any time. For example, you may have to add points to express the general idea for a group of details, or you may have to add details to explain and develop a certain point.
- Draw a line through any ideas that do not support your main idea.

See the example in Chapter 4, page 80.

MAKING A ROUGH OUTLINE

Many writers find this technique the easiest and most effective way to organize their ideas. Generally, an outline follows this basic pattern:

```
                          OUTLINE

Main idea _____

Body
     Point 1  _____

        Details _____

     Point 2  _____

        Details _____

     Point 3  _____

        Details _____

Conclusion  _____
```

Write key words, phrases, and ideas on the blank lines. Leave out any ideas that do not contribute to an effective composition. You can find more specific outline suggestions in the individual chapters.

Step 3: Writing the First Draft

Using the information from the first two steps, you will write your first draft. In the first draft, you should focus on content and organization, and worry about grammar later, in the second or final draft.

While you are writing, you may find that you are satisfied with your plan. In many cases, however, you will discover that you want to make changes. You may make changes at any time, but first make sure that your new plan is well organized.

An excellent way to check your new plan for effective organization is to write out a new rough outline and evaluate it carefully before you continue.

Step 4: Revising

Revising means improving the content and organization of your draft. After you complete an early draft, it will be much easier to analyze it to see how well your ideas fit together. Even if you are happy with your draft, you can usually find ways to improve it.

When you revise, you can add material, eliminate material, or move material from one spot to another. Use any system you wish to make your revisions clear to yourself.

Check the main idea. Is it complete, with a clear topic and comment? Is it appropriate for the body and conclusion?

Next, check the body for support. Do you need to add more details? Should you eliminate an idea that doesn't fit as well as you thought it did at first? Perhaps the idea you need to eliminate is irrelevant, or too vague, or too general. Do you need to move material from one spot to another? Have you included helpful signals to guide the reader from idea to idea?

Finally, check your conclusion. Does it tie the entire composition together and give closure?

Keep in mind that successful writers, even professional writers, routinely revise and improve on their early drafts. See the example in Chapter 1, page 14.

PEER RESPONSE

Most often, writers cannot see their own strengths and weaknesses as clearly as someone else can. Getting input from others, then, is an extremely useful activity.

In addition to benefiting from useful input from your partner, peer response also helps you when you read and analyze your partner's composition for improvement. It does this by helping you develop the skills that you need to revise your own compositions effectively.

When you work with a partner, comment on your partner's success in communicating the content effectively. Are the ideas clear, well organized, and convincing? Are there any spots that are hard to understand? Be honest! Your comments will help your partner.

Of course, you and your partner must make the final decisions about what to change (or not to change) in your own drafts.

See the specific instructions in each corresponding chapter.

SELF-EVALUATION

In this activity, you will analyze your own draft for ways to improve the content and organization. The best way to do this is to set your draft aside for at least twenty-four hours so that you can evaluate it with a fresh mind.

See the specific instructions in each corresponding chapter.

Step 5: Proofreading and Editing

Proofreading means looking for errors. Editing means correcting the errors. (Some people use these terms interchangeably.)

In this step, you will proofread and edit your draft for errors in grammar and visual presentation. When you edit, you can cross out any material you want to eliminate, add words, or correct any other errors.

PEER RESPONSE

As noted earlier for Peer Response, most often writers cannot see their own strengths and weaknesses as clearly as someone else can.

Similar to peer revising, this activity provides you with useful input from your partner to help you edit your own draft. Also, it gives you valuable practice in proofreading.

Of course, you and your partner must make the final decisions about what to change (or not to change) in your own drafts.

See the specific instructions in each corresponding chapter.

SELF-EVALUATION

For this activity, you will proofread and edit your own draft. Look for the kinds of grammar errors you know you tend to make in your writing. If you're not sure what your own personal weakness are, check the instructor's notes on your past writing assignments. If you're still not sure, ask your instructor.

The best way to proofread and edit is to set your draft aside for at least twenty-four hours before you check it. By giving yourself a day, you will be able to evaluate it with a fresh mind. See the specific instructions in each corresponding chapter.

Note: Some instructors combine both revising and editing in the same peer-response activity. Other instructors limit peer response to revising only. Make sure you understand which method your instructor prefers.

Step 6: Writing the Final Draft

If you've done the previous steps carefully, this is the easiest step of all. All you have to do is rewrite your draft with the revisions and corrections.

After you finish, proofread and edit your draft again carefully. If, however, you have more than a few errors to correct, or if the changes consist of more than a few letters or a word or two here and there, you should rewrite the entire draft.

Remember, too, that this is the time to make sure your composition makes a good visual impression. Visual impressions are important, in the same way that what you wear to a job interview is important! Follow the guidelines given in class for visual presentation.

Step 7: Following Up and Evaluating Progress

SHARING YOUR WRITING WITH OTHERS

You have put a lot of time and effort into writing your composition. The product of your efforts deserves to be read — not only by your instructor, but by your classmates and others as well.

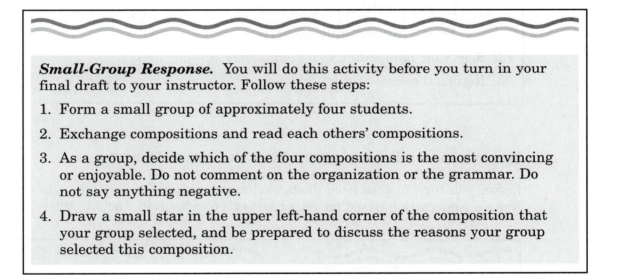

Small-Group Response. You will do this activity before you turn in your final draft to your instructor. Follow these steps:

1. Form a small group of approximately four students.

2. Exchange compositions and read each others' compositions.

3. As a group, decide which of the four compositions is the most convincing or enjoyable. Do not comment on the organization or the grammar. Do not say anything negative.

4. Draw a small star in the upper left-hand corner of the composition that your group selected, and be prepared to discuss the reasons your group selected this composition.

Traveling Compositions. You will do this activity before you turn in your final draft to the instructor. Follow these steps:

1. Exchange compositions with a classmate. Repeat this step with another classmate. Repeat it several more times. In this way, your composition will "travel" across the classroom.

2. Read the composition that "traveled" into your hands.

3. At the end of the composition, write a positive comment — a sentence or two — about the content.

> Possible comments:
>
> I enjoyed reading your ideas.
>
> I have a similar point of view.
>
> I've had an experience like yours.
>
> You've really convinced me about . . .
>
> I admire your. . .
>
> I like. . .
>
> Do not comment on organization or grammar.
>
> Do not say anything negative.

4. Sign your name after your comment.

5. Return the composition.

WINDING DOWN: RESPONDING TO YOUR CLASSMATES' WRITING

Before you turn in your final draft, exchange compositions with a classmate, and write a composition based on your partner's composition. Include the following:

1. A statement to identify your partner's composition

2. A summary of the most important ideas

3. A response: your ideas or opinions, based on the ideas in the composition

See the example in Chapter 3, page 64.

BENEFITING FROM FEEDBACK

After your instructor returns your composition to you, make sure you understand your patterns of strengths and weaknesses.

Congratulate yourself for your strengths. You've worked hard, and you deserve to give yourself credit for your progress.

Keep a list of weaknesses or errors. The following is one way to chart your progress:

Content and Organization	*Grammar*
Writing Assignment (WA)	
WA 1 _____	_____
WA 2 _____	_____
WA 3 _____	_____

By keeping a record of your progress over a period of time, you can identify your strengths and weaknesses. Then you can develop a plan of independent study, focusing on improving your weaknesses.

Final Advice for Process Writing

Good writers follow these steps as closely as possible, making some adjustments for the type of assignment they are doing.

In certain cases, however, it may be difficult or even impossible for you to follow all of the steps thoroughly. For example, for an in-class writing assignment, you will have to use a much briefer version of the process than you would for a take-home composition.

Even for take-home compositions, you may decide not to follow the steps exactly as they are presented. Instead, you may decide to do certain steps at the same time, or you may want to return to an earlier step.

The point is that writing situations differ, and personal styles differ as well. In time and with practice, you will adapt these steps to your own personal style and situation.

Your Personal Spelling List

The most effective way to improve your spelling is for you to keep a personal spelling list. Every time you find a word that you have had difficulty spelling and you will probably use again in the future, write the correct spelling on your Personal Spelling List. Periodically, review and practice the words on this list.

studying

writing

written

Grammar Highlights

Including a Subject and a Verb in Every Sentence

In academic writing, every sentence must contain at least one subject and one verb.

THE SUBJECT

The subject tells what the sentence is about. The subject can be a noun or a pronoun. Read this sample, and notice the different kinds of subjects.

> I interviewed Zahid Memon in my ESL writing class this semester. Zahid is from Pakistan. He came to this country two years ago in January. His uncle picked him up from the airport.

There is a special class of subjects called "filler subjects." Filler subjects consist of *it* and *there*.

> It was a cloudy, rainy evening when Zahib arrived. It was very cold. There was a lot of traffic on the freeway because there had been several accidents.

THE VERB

The verb supplies the action or state of being for the subject. A verb may consist of one word or several words (one or more auxiliaries plus the main verb). Notice the different verb forms in the following paragraphs:

> The following Saturday, Zahib's aunt and uncle took him to see the sights in the city. They showed him the beautiful buildings in the financial district. They also spent some time at Stanley Park. Zahid was very impressed.
>
> Now, two years later, Zahid has seen a lot of tourist spots. To give a few examples, he has visited Niagara Falls, Banff National Park, and New York City. Also, he has been saving his money for a trip to Las Vegas, Nevada.

PRACTICE

Identify the subjects and verbs in ten sentences from one of your recent writing assignments. For each sentence, underline under the subject once and the verb twice.

Understanding Clauses

A clause is a group of related words with (at least) one subject and verb. Read the following examples:

- Zahib plays the cello.   S   +   V

- Zahib and his sister play
  in an orchestra.   S + S   +   V

- Zahib practices his cello and
  does his school work on the weekends.   S   +   V + V

- Zahib and his sister love music
  and plan to major in music.   S + S   +   V + V

An *independent clause* can stand alone as a sentence. All the examples above are independent clauses.

A *dependent clause* cannot stand alone as a sentence. It is usually introduced by a *subordinator*.

Common Subordinators

Time:	*Contrast:*	*Condition:*	*Cause/Effect:*
when	although	if	because
before	though	unless	since
after	even though		
while			
as soon as			
until			
just as			

After Zahib gets his undergraduate degree in music, . . .

Even though Zahib's sister wants to major in music, . . .

If Zahib gets into a master's program at the university, . . .

. . . because Zahib loves music so much.

PRACTICE

In one of your recent writing assignments, identify five independent clauses and five dependent clauses. Underline the independent clauses and double underline the dependent clauses.

I really miss my parents because I haven't seen them for almost a year.

As soon as this semester is over, I'll visit my family.

Understanding Sentence Types

The three basic sentence types consist of the following:

Simple sentence:	Last semester I had an embarrassing experience with the campus police.
Compound sentence:	I unintentionally parked illegally, and a student cadet gave me a ticket.
Complex sentence:	When I saw him put the ticket on my windshield, I panicked.

1. SIMPLE SENTENCES

The following are *simple sentences* consisting of one independent clause.

He looked like a robber to me.
I ran toward him.
He saw me and didn't move.

2. COMPOUND SENTENCES

The following are *compound sentences*. They contain two independent clauses. There is usually a comma and a *coordinator* between the clauses. Common coordinators include *and, but*, and *so*.

I yelled, and he turned toward me.
I still didn't understand the situation, so I kept yelling.
Finally I saw his uniform, and I got embarrassed.
I apologized, but I still felt ridiculous.

3. COMPLEX SENTENCES

Complex sentences contain one independent clause and one or more dependent clauses.

Even though I didn't intend to park illegally, I still felt like a criminal.
I was at fault because I reacted without thinking.
When I remember that day, I get embarrassed all over again.
If I see that cadet again, I'll hide my face.

 **PRACTICE**

Think of an embarrassing situation you have had. Write several sentences about the situation, and identify the sentences according to their type: simple (S), compound (CD), or complex (CX). Write S, CD, or CX in the margin.

Avoiding Run-on Sentences

A run-on sentence is an error. It consists of two (or more) independent clauses without correct punctuation between them.

Run-on Sentences

My neighborhood has a block party every year, we usually have it the last weekend of summer.

It takes a lot of planning we all work together to make it happen.

First, we decide who is going to be responsible for what, I usually get permission from the city, it's not that difficult to do.

Corrected Run-on Sentences

My neighborhood has a block party every year. We usually have it the last weekend of summer.

(Or: My neighborhood has a block party the last weekend of every summer.)

It takes a lot of planning, but we all work together to make it happen.

First, we decide who is going to be responsible for what. I usually get permission from the city. It's not that difficult to do.

 **PRACTICE**

Identify run-on sentences from past writing assignments. On a separate piece of paper, rewrite them correctly.

Avoiding Sentence Fragments

Each sentence must contain at least one independent clause, and each clause must contain a subject and a verb.

Sentence Fragments

(*Note:* In each example, the second group of words forms a sentence fragment.)

1. A. I go to city hall as soon as it opens in the morning.
   B. Because the lines are shorter at that time.

2. A. The clerk gives me an application to fill out.
   B. Also, a list of the rules that we must follow.

3. A. I get signatures from my neighbors.
   B. And return the application to city hall. The next day.

Corrected Sentence Fragments

1. I go to city hall as soon as it opens in the morning because the lines are shorter at that time.
2. The clerk gives me an application to fill out. Also, he gives me a list of the rules that we must follow. (Or: The clerk gives me an application to fill out and a list of the rules we must follow.)
3. I get signatures from my neighbors and return the application to city hall the next day.

 **PRACTICE**

Identify sentence fragments from past writing assignments. On a separate piece of paper, write corrections for the fragments.

Using the Present Tense

The two most common uses of the present tense are for habitual action and general truth.

> My roommate Sima <u>studies</u> a lot for tests. First, she <u>outlines</u> all her texts and class notes, focusing on points the instructor has stressed in class. Then, she <u>writes</u> study questions for herself. After that, she <u>makes</u> flash cards to quiz herself. It's no wonder that she always <u>gets</u> A's on her tests.

Note: A common error students make is to forget to use the "s" form of the present tense for a third-person singular subject.

 **PRACTICE**

Write several sentences about a friend. Tell what's generally true about him or her and what he or she does habitually. Underline the present tense verbs, and make sure the third-person verbs have an "s."

Using the Past Tense

The most common use of the past tense is for action or state of being in the past.

> At dinner last night my roommate <u>dripped</u> spaghetti onto her pants. Then she <u>spilled</u> her juice on the tablecloth. After that, on her way to the kitchen with the bread basket, she <u>tripped</u> on an electric cord and <u>dropped</u> the bread on the floor. By 9:30, she <u>decided</u> to go to bed early in order to avoid more accidents.

 **PRACTICE**

Write an imaginary story about a person who had a bad day. Underline the past tense verbs.

Acknowledgments

It is a violation of the law to reproduce these selections by any means whatsoever without the written permission of the copyright holder.

Excerpt from *Chicken Soup for the Soul* by Jack Canfield and Mark V. Hansen. Copyright © 1993. Reprinted with permission of Health Communications, Inc.

Jose M. Tingson. "Culture Shock Result of Many Small Things." Published in WARWHOOP, April 20-27, 1989. Reprinted by permission of the author.

Excerpt from *Shizuko's Daughter* by Kyoko Mori. Copyright © 1993 by Kyoko Mori. Reprinted by permission of Henry Holt & Co.

Excerpt from *April and the Dragon Lady* by Lensey Namioka. Copyright © 1994 by Lensey Namioka. Reprinted by permission of Harcourt Brace & Company and Ruth Cohen, Inc., agent for the author.

"Another Evening at the Club" from *Arabic Short Stories*, edited and translated by Denys Johnson-Davies. Copyright © 1983 by Denys Johnson-Davies. Published by Quartet Books Ltd. Reprinted by permission of the publisher.

Excerpt from *Paradise of the Blind* by Duong Thu Huong. Copyright © 1988 by Duong Thu Huong. First published in the USA by William Morrow and Company, Inc. Reprinted by permission.

David Nava Monreal. "Sister Katherine." Copyright © 1991 David Monreal. Reprinted by permission of the author.

brainstorm controversial topics

:

Int Writ Activity?